SAMSUNG GALAXY S25 ULTRA
USER GUIDE

Navigating the Interface with Ease

KATE T. RANDY

COPYRIGHT

TABLE OF CONTENTS

COPYRIGHT... 1

TABLE OF CONTENTS 2

INTRODUCTION 4

The Future of Smartphones with the Samsung Galaxy S25 Ultra 4

CHAPTER 1 12

Samsung Galaxy S25 Ultra 12

CHAPTER 2 21

The Genesis of the Galaxy S Series 21

CHAPTER 3 30

Unveiling the Galaxy S25 Ultra 30

CHAPTER 4 40

Design and Build Quality 40

CHAPTER 5 50

Performance and Hardware 50

CHAPTER 6 61

Camera Capabilities 61

CHAPTER 7 73

Software and User Interface 73

CHAPTER 8 85

Awards and Recognitions 85

CHAPTER 9 96

Current Challenges and Market Position 96

CHAPTER 10 107

The Future of the Galaxy S Series............................ 107

CONCLUSION..118

The Samsung Galaxy S25 Ultra – A Benchmark in Smartphone Innovation...118

INTRODUCTION

The Future of Smartphones with the Samsung Galaxy S25 Ultra

In the fast-paced world of technology, smartphones have become the focal point of our daily lives. We rely on them for communication, work, entertainment, photography, and countless other functions. As the digital landscape continues to evolve, so too do the devices we depend on. At the forefront of this evolution is Samsung, a company that has consistently redefined the smartphone experience with each iteration of its flagship Galaxy series. Among its most recent groundbreaking offerings is the Samsung Galaxy S25 Ultra, a device that promises to take smartphone innovation to new heights.

This book is dedicated to exploring every aspect of the Samsung Galaxy S25 Ultra, from its design and performance to the cutting-edge technologies that make it stand out in a crowded market. Whether you're a tech enthusiast, a potential buyer, or simply someone interested in the future of mobile technology, this book will provide you with a comprehensive and human-centered perspective on what makes the Galaxy S25 Ultra one of the most anticipated smartphones of 2025.

The Evolution of the Galaxy Series: A Brief History

Samsung's Galaxy S series has been a significant force in shaping the smartphone industry. Since the release of the original Galaxy S in 2010, the brand has consistently raised the bar for mobile technology. With each new model, Samsung has introduced innovations that push the boundaries of what is possible in a smartphone. Features like large, high-resolution displays, powerful processors, versatile cameras, and cutting-edge software have made the Galaxy S series a favorite among consumers worldwide.

The journey from the Galaxy S to the S25 Ultra has been one of constant reinvention. Early models focused heavily on display quality, with Samsung's AMOLED technology becoming a defining feature. As smartphones evolved, the Galaxy S series integrated more advanced features like wireless charging, multi-lens camera systems, and, most recently, AI-powered functionalities that enhance user experience.

The Galaxy S25 Ultra represents the pinnacle of Samsung's efforts in the smartphone space. With its advanced hardware, sophisticated software, and innovative design, it is a device that reflects both the brand's legacy and its future. But what makes the Galaxy S25 Ultra stand out from its predecessors? And why has it generated so much excitement in the tech community?

The Galaxy S25 Ultra: A Technological Masterpiece

The Samsung Galaxy S25 Ultra is not just another smartphone; it is a device that integrates advanced technologies designed to improve the user experience across various aspects. From the very first moment you hold it in your hands, the S25 Ultra feels different. Its design is sleek yet robust, and the premium materials used in its construction, including a titanium frame and Gorilla Armor 2 glass, give it an air of sophistication and durability.

But the real magic lies inside. The Galaxy S25 Ultra is powered by the Qualcomm Snapdragon 8 Elite processor, which offers a significant boost in performance compared to its predecessors. This cutting-edge chipset, combined with an impressive 12GB of RAM, ensures that the device can handle even the most demanding tasks with ease, whether it's playing graphics-intensive games, multitasking with multiple apps, or editing 4K video.

Perhaps one of the most impressive features of the Galaxy S25 Ultra is its camera system. With a 200MP wide-angle lens, a 50MP ultra-wide lens, and a 10MP periscope telephoto lens that supports 5x optical zoom, this smartphone is capable of capturing stunning images and videos with exceptional clarity and detail. Whether you're shooting landscapes, portraits, or action shots, the Galaxy S25 Ultra's camera system delivers impressive results every time.

The display is another standout feature of the Galaxy S25 Ultra. Samsung's Dynamic LTPO AMOLED 2X screen offers a 120Hz refresh rate and a 3120x1440 pixel resolution, making it ideal for everything from gaming to streaming high-definition videos. The screen's color accuracy and brightness levels are exceptional, ensuring that every image on your device looks vibrant and true-to-life.

A Deep Dive into the Features

In the following chapters, we will dive deeper into the various features that make the Galaxy S25 Ultra an exceptional device. You'll discover how the smartphone's AI integration enhances everyday tasks, how the Active Noise Cancellation (ANC) feature improves your listening experience, and how the Personalized Spatial Audio technology provides an immersive sound experience like no other.

We will also explore the device's battery life and charging capabilities, both of which have been improved significantly compared to earlier models. With a 5000mAh battery and support for 45W wired charging and 15W wireless charging, the Galaxy S25 Ultra ensures that you can go through your day without worrying about running out of power. Furthermore, its ability to seamlessly switch between devices with dual-device connectivity makes it ideal for users who frequently switch between their smartphones, tablets, and laptops.

One of the most notable advancements in the Galaxy S25 Ultra is the inclusion of Samsung's One UI 7, an intuitive and user-friendly operating system built on Android 15. With Galaxy AI, the S25 Ultra learns from your habits, helping automate tasks and suggesting actions based on your preferences. The software also integrates with Samsung's SmartThings ecosystem, allowing you to control your smart home devices directly from the phone.

Family Background: The Samsung Legacy

Samsung's roots date back to 1938, when it was founded as a trading company by Lee Byung-chul in South Korea. The company has since grown into one of the world's largest and most influential conglomerates, with a presence in numerous industries including electronics, construction, and entertainment. However, it is in the field of technology, particularly consumer electronics, where Samsung has made its mark as a global leader.

Samsung Electronics, a subsidiary of Samsung Group, is the division responsible for the development of the Galaxy S series. The company's innovative culture, along with its massive investment in research and development, has allowed it to stay ahead of competitors in the rapidly changing smartphone market. As of 2025, Samsung continues to dominate the global smartphone market, with the Galaxy S25 Ultra being one of its most significant offerings to date.

The Family of Samsung Smartphones

The Galaxy S25 Ultra is not the only device in Samsung's Galaxy S series, but it is certainly the most advanced. It sits at the top of a lineup that includes the Galaxy S25 and the Galaxy S25 Plus, each offering a slightly different feature set to cater to various user preferences and budgets. While the S25 Ultra represents the cutting edge of smartphone technology, the S25 and S25 Plus provide more affordable alternatives without compromising on quality or performance.

Challenges and the Road Ahead

Despite its many innovations, the Galaxy S25 Ultra faces challenges that reflect the broader smartphone industry. Competition remains fierce, with companies like Apple, Google, and Xiaomi pushing the envelope in terms of design, functionality, and price. Additionally, global supply chain disruptions and geopolitical tensions have posed challenges for manufacturers like Samsung, impacting production and availability.

Samsung is also navigating the increasingly saturated market for high-end smartphones, where customers have become more discerning and less willing to upgrade their devices every year. As a result, Samsung must continue to innovate while maintaining affordability to ensure the Galaxy S series remains a top choice for consumers.

Looking ahead, Samsung is focused on improving the integration of AI technologies, enhancing 5G capabilities, and exploring the future of foldable and rollable screens. These advancements will shape the direction of the Galaxy series in the coming years, and it will be exciting to see how the Galaxy S25 Ultra paves the way for the future of mobile technology.

The Galaxy S25 Ultra and the Future of Smartphones

The Samsung Galaxy S25 Ultra is more than just a smartphone; it is a testament to Samsung's commitment to innovation and its vision for the future of mobile technology. With its advanced hardware, sophisticated software, and cutting-edge features, it is a device that sets the standard for what modern smartphones can achieve.

This book aims to take you on a journey through the features, history, and potential of the Galaxy S25 Ultra, offering a deep dive into what makes this device one of the most anticipated smartphones of 2025. Whether you're a tech enthusiast eager to learn about the latest advancements, a potential buyer weighing the pros and cons, or simply someone fascinated by the evolution of smartphones, the Galaxy S25 Ultra is sure to leave a lasting impression.

So, let's dive in and explore everything that makes the Samsung Galaxy S25 Ultra a true marvel of modern technology.

CHAPTER 1
Samsung Galaxy S25 Ultra

1.1 Overview of the Samsung Galaxy S25 Ultra

In the realm of high-end smartphones, Samsung has long been a dominant player, constantly pushing the envelope of what we expect from mobile devices. As one of the most prominent names in the technology sector, Samsung continues to innovate with each iteration of its flagship Galaxy S series, and the **Samsung Galaxy S25 Ultra** is no exception. Unveiled in January 2025, this smartphone sets a new benchmark for premium mobile devices, blending cutting-edge technology, elegant design, and impressive functionality in one package.

The **Samsung Galaxy S25 Ultra** features a **6.9-inch Dynamic LTPO AMOLED 2X** display with a **120Hz refresh rate**, offering users an immersive viewing experience that is ideal for everything from watching high-definition videos to gaming and browsing. The screen resolution of **3120x1440 pixels** ensures that every image is crisp and vibrant, showcasing the beauty of Samsung's commitment to display excellence. The phone is also equipped with a **Snapdragon 8 Elite processor**, making it one of the most powerful smartphones available in terms of performance. With up to **12GB of RAM** and **1TB of storage** available, the S25 Ultra ensures users can multitask and store their data with ease.

At the heart of this smartphone lies a camera system that redefines mobile photography. With a **200MP wide-angle lens**, a **50MP ultra-wide lens**, and a **10MP telephoto lens** that supports up to **5x optical zoom**, this device is designed to capture stunning images and videos with unrivaled detail. Samsung's camera technology continues to improve with each iteration, and the S25 Ultra is the culmination of years of refinement, boasting advanced features like **AI-powered enhancements**, **adaptive image stabilization**, and **improved low-light performance**. Whether you are a professional photographer or an everyday user, the camera system on the Galaxy S25 Ultra offers a versatile and high-quality photography experience.

Another key feature that sets the Galaxy S25 Ultra apart is its **battery life**. Equipped with a **5000mAh battery**, the device supports **45W wired charging** and **15W wireless charging**, ensuring that users can charge their phones quickly and efficiently. The battery is also optimized for long-lasting performance, allowing users to enjoy a full day of use even with demanding apps and features.

The Galaxy S25 Ultra runs on **Android 15** with **Samsung's One UI 7**, which provides an intuitive and user-friendly interface. With features like **Galaxy AI**, the phone learns from your habits to enhance your overall experience by offering smart suggestions and automating routine tasks. This seamless integration of hardware and software is one of the reasons why the S25 Ultra stands out as a true flagship device.

In addition to its impressive performance, the S25 Ultra offers **5G connectivity**, ensuring users can access faster data speeds and more reliable connections. Whether you are streaming videos, downloading files, or playing online games, the 5G capability enhances the phone's performance, making it one of the most future-proof devices on the market.

Design and Build Quality
The **Samsung Galaxy S25 Ultra** features a premium design with **Titanium Armor** framing and **Gorilla Armor 2 glass** on the front and back, making the device not only stunning but incredibly durable. It comes in a range of sophisticated color options, including **Titanium Silverblue**, **Titanium**

Black, and **Titanium Gray**, with exclusive online colors like **Titanium Jetblack** and **Titanium Jadegreen**. The device's slim profile and ergonomic design ensure a comfortable grip while maintaining a sleek, modern aesthetic. Its **IP68 rating** means that the S25 Ultra is resistant to dust and water, further enhancing its durability.

Overall, the Samsung Galaxy S25 Ultra is not just a smartphone; it's a powerhouse device that combines advanced technology with a stunning design. It is a reflection of Samsung's dedication to innovation and its pursuit of creating the ultimate mobile experience for users across the globe.

1.2 Purpose of the Book

The purpose of this book is to provide a comprehensive guide to the **Samsung Galaxy S25 Ultra**, covering all aspects of the device, from its design and hardware to its software features and advanced functionalities. Whether you are a first-time Galaxy user, a long-time Samsung fan, or someone who is considering upgrading to the Galaxy S25 Ultra, this book will serve as an essential resource for understanding the full capabilities of the device.

The **Samsung Galaxy S25 Ultra** is an impressive and complex smartphone, packed with numerous features that can be overwhelming to many users. This book aims to break down those features in a clear and accessible way, ensuring that readers can fully appreciate the device's potential. By the end of this guide, you will be well-equipped to make the most out of your S25 Ultra, whether you are using it for productivity, entertainment, photography, or simply staying connected with others.

The book will explore the various aspects of the Galaxy S25 Ultra in detail, offering insights into its hardware, software, camera system, connectivity, and much more. Through step-by-step guides, expert tips, and troubleshooting advice, this book aims to help readers understand how to maximize the performance of their device and use it in the most efficient and effective way possible.

The goal of this book is to cater to both tech enthusiasts and everyday users. While some sections will delve into the technical aspects of the device, there will also be user-friendly explanations and practical tips for those who may not be as familiar with smartphone technology. Whether you're a seasoned smartphone user or a novice, this guide will offer something for everyone.

Furthermore, the book will provide insights into the Samsung Galaxy S25 Ultra's future-proof features. With its advanced hardware, 5G capabilities, and AI-powered enhancements, the S25 Ultra is designed to remain relevant for years to come. This guide will not only show you how to use your device today but will also help you understand how it will evolve and adapt to new technologies in the future.

Ultimately, the purpose of this book is to empower readers to unlock the full potential of the Samsung Galaxy S25 Ultra. From basic setup instructions to in-depth tutorials on the most advanced features, this book will serve as your trusted companion as you navigate the world of Samsung's flagship smartphone.

1.3 How to Use This Book

This book is organized to help you easily navigate the many features and capabilities of the **Samsung Galaxy S25 Ultra**. Each chapter is designed to focus on specific aspects of the device, providing a structured and logical flow that will guide you from the basics of setting up your phone to mastering the most advanced features.

The **first section** of the book covers the fundamentals, including setting up the device, understanding the user interface, and learning how to navigate the basic functions of the phone. This section is ideal for those who are new to Samsung smartphones or those upgrading from an older model. It will provide you with the necessary knowledge to get started with your Galaxy S25 Ultra and ensure you're comfortable using it from the outset.

The **second section** delves into more advanced topics, such as the camera system, battery management, and software features. Here, you will learn how to take full advantage of the S25 Ultra's impressive camera capabilities, from capturing stunning photos to recording professional-quality video. We'll also discuss how to optimize battery life and ensure that your phone runs efficiently throughout the day.

The **third section** explores the most cutting-edge features of the Galaxy S25 Ultra, such as **AI integration**, **5G connectivity**, and **Personalized Spatial Audio**. This section will teach you how to use these features to enhance your overall experience, whether you are using the phone for productivity, entertainment, or gaming.

Each chapter of this book includes step-by-step guides, practical tips, and real-world examples to help you better understand how to use the Galaxy S25 Ultra. Wherever necessary, we provide troubleshooting advice to help you resolve common issues that may arise during use. Additionally, at the end of each chapter, you will find a

summary and **FAQs** that provide quick answers to common questions and important points to remember.

In addition to the main content, this book features **appendices** that provide technical specifications, a glossary of terms, and further reading materials for those who want to dive deeper into specific topics related to the Galaxy S25 Ultra. These sections serve as useful reference points for readers who wish to explore more detailed aspects of the device or learn about related technologies.

This book is designed to be user-friendly and accessible. Whether you are a casual user who wants to learn how to use your phone more effectively or a tech enthusiast looking to explore all the possibilities of the Galaxy S25 Ultra, this guide is structured to provide the right balance of in-depth information and easy-to-understand explanations.

To make the most of this book, we recommend reading it from start to finish if you are new to the Galaxy S25 Ultra, as this will give you a comprehensive understanding of all its features. However, if you are already familiar with the basics of smartphone usage, you can skip to the sections that interest you the most and use the index to find specific topics.

This book also encourages hands-on learning. As you follow along with the tutorials and guides, we suggest that you try out the features on your own phone, as this will help reinforce your learning and ensure that you are comfortable using the device in real-world scenarios.

By the end of this book, you will have a thorough understanding of everything the **Samsung Galaxy S25 Ultra** has to offer. You'll be able to take full advantage of its advanced features, optimize its performance, and solve any issues that arise. Whether you are a novice or an experienced smartphone user, this book will serve as your ultimate guide to mastering the **Samsung Galaxy S25 Ultra**.

CHAPTER 2

The Genesis of the Galaxy S Series

Samsung's rise in the smartphone industry has been nothing short of spectacular. From its early days in the consumer electronics market to its current position as one of the global leaders in mobile technology, Samsung has continually shaped the direction of smartphone design and functionality. At the heart of its success is the **Galaxy S series**, a line of devices that has become synonymous with innovation and premium quality. This chapter delves into the journey of Samsung's entry into the smartphone market, the evolution of the Galaxy S lineup, and the milestones that led to the creation of the **Samsung Galaxy S25 Ultra**, the latest and most advanced flagship smartphone in the series.

2.1 Samsung's Entry into the Smartphone Market

Before it became the giant it is today, Samsung was primarily known for its expertise in consumer electronics, particularly televisions and home appliances. However, as the mobile industry began to grow in the late 1990s and early 2000s, Samsung recognized the need to expand its focus into mobile phones. By the mid-2000s, the company was already manufacturing mobile phones, but they were not yet the premium devices that would define its future.

Samsung's initial foray into the mobile phone market was marked by a focus on **feature phones**, which dominated the landscape during that era. These phones were functional but lacked the sophisticated features that would later become synonymous with smartphones. However, as the smartphone revolution began to unfold with the introduction of the **Apple iPhone** in 2007, Samsung quickly realized that the future of mobile phones lay in the convergence of multiple functions—communication, entertainment, photography, and computing—into a single device. The iPhone, with its sleek touchscreen interface and powerful capabilities, demonstrated the potential of smartphones to revolutionize the way people interacted with technology.

Recognizing the rapid shift in the market, Samsung pivoted its focus to the development of smartphones that would compete with Apple's groundbreaking device. In 2009, the company made a strategic decision to design its own smartphones, ultimately introducing its first Android-powered phone, the **Samsung Galaxy**. This move marked the beginning of Samsung's serious commitment to the smartphone market, and it laid the foundation for the **Galaxy**

S series that would become a cornerstone of the company's mobile strategy.

2.2 Evolution of the Galaxy S Lineup

The introduction of the **Galaxy S series** in 2010 was a pivotal moment for Samsung, as it marked the company's entry into the high-end smartphone market. The first **Samsung Galaxy S** model set the tone for the brand's future success, combining high-end hardware with the then-new Android operating system. The device featured a **4-inch Super AMOLED display**, which was a standout feature at the time for its vibrant colors and deep blacks. This was a clear statement of Samsung's commitment to producing devices with top-tier displays, a hallmark that would remain throughout the evolution of the Galaxy S lineup.

The early years of the Galaxy S series were focused on refining the core features that would define the brand: premium display quality, powerful performance, and robust cameras. With each new iteration, Samsung introduced significant upgrades, adding new features and improving existing ones. The **Galaxy S2** (2011) introduced a slimmer design and improved performance, while the **Galaxy S3** (2012) featured a larger screen and better camera capabilities, cementing Samsung's reputation as a top-tier smartphone manufacturer.

Galaxy S4 (2013) pushed the boundaries further with its **5-inch Full HD display**, solidifying Samsung's commitment to large, high-quality screens. This model also introduced **Air Gesture** and **Smart Scroll**, features that allowed users to interact with the phone without physically touching it, demonstrating Samsung's focus on innovative user experience.

With the launch of the **Galaxy S5** (2014), Samsung took another leap forward by introducing a **water-resistant design**, a feature that was becoming increasingly popular as consumers sought more durable devices. The S5 also introduced **fingerprint recognition** for added security, positioning Samsung as a leader in mobile technology.

One of the most significant milestones in the evolution of the Galaxy S series came with the release of the **Galaxy S6** (2015). This model marked a major departure from its predecessors with a **premium glass and metal design** and the introduction of **fast charging** technology. The Galaxy S6 Edge, with its curved display, was a game-changer, offering a new visual and functional experience that would later become a hallmark of Samsung's flagship phones.

Samsung continued to innovate with the **Galaxy S7** (2016), which brought back the water resistance feature and improved the camera further. The **S8** (2017) introduced the **Infinity Display**, a nearly bezel-less screen that stretched from edge to edge, marking a radical departure from traditional smartphone design. This shift to a nearly full-screen design would become a defining feature of Samsung's smartphones for years to come.

The **Galaxy S9** (2018) focused on enhancing the camera capabilities with a dual-aperture lens, enabling better low-light performance. The **S10** series (2019) introduced the **punch-hole camera** and **ultrasonic fingerprint sensor**, offering a more immersive experience with a sleek design and cutting-edge features.

By the time the **Galaxy S20** series (2020) was released, Samsung had fully embraced 5G technology, and the phones in this lineup were among the first to offer 5G connectivity to consumers. This marked the beginning of the next chapter in Samsung's quest for innovation, positioning the Galaxy S series as a device for future-proofing, ready for the fast-paced advancements in wireless technology.

The **Galaxy S21** series (2021) refined the design and functionality even further, incorporating a **camera bump**

design that was more integrated into the phone's overall structure, while the **S22** and **S23** series (2022-2023) continued to enhance the cameras and performance, with improvements in **AI-driven features** and overall user experience.

Throughout this evolution, Samsung's Galaxy S lineup remained at the forefront of smartphone innovation, consistently introducing new features and refining existing ones to meet the needs and desires of its ever-growing customer base. Each iteration of the Galaxy S series built on the foundation laid by its predecessors, resulting in a device that is both a **powerhouse of performance** and a **symbol of cutting-edge technology**.

2.3 Milestones Leading to the Galaxy S25 Ultra

The **Samsung Galaxy S25 Ultra** represents the culmination of over a decade of smartphone innovation. It is not just a phone; it is a device that incorporates years of advancements in mobile technology, design, and user experience. The journey leading to the Galaxy S25 Ultra is marked by several key milestones, each one contributing to the development of this exceptional smartphone.

1.   The   Rise   of   the   Curved   Display
One of the most defining features of Samsung smartphones

over the past few years has been the **curved display**. First introduced with the **Galaxy S6 Edge**, the curved screen quickly became a signature feature of the Galaxy S lineup, offering a more immersive and visually striking experience. Over the years, Samsung has continued to refine the curved display, making it a key component of its flagship devices. By the time the **S25 Ultra** was introduced, the curved screen had become a standard, not only providing aesthetic appeal but also adding functionality with features like **edge screen shortcuts** and **dual-edge display features**.

2.   The   Introduction   of   5G   Connectivity

As 5G technology began to roll out globally, Samsung made it a priority to integrate **5G connectivity** into its smartphones. The **Galaxy S20** series was one of the first to offer **5G compatibility**, allowing users to take advantage of faster speeds and more reliable connections. With the **S25 Ultra**, Samsung has taken 5G connectivity to the next level, ensuring that the device is future-proof and capable of handling the increasing demand for high-speed data transfer.

3.   Advancements   in   Mobile   Photography

Samsung has always prided itself on its camera technology, and the Galaxy S series has been at the forefront of mobile photography innovations. From the early days of the **Galaxy**

S4 with its 13MP camera to the **200MP wide-angle lens** in the **S25 Ultra**, Samsung has consistently pushed the boundaries of mobile photography. The **S25 Ultra's** camera system is a testament to this evolution, featuring multiple lenses, advanced AI-powered software, and improved low-light capabilities, making it one of the best smartphones for photography on the market.

4. The Integration of Artificial Intelligence
In recent years, Samsung has increasingly relied on **artificial intelligence (AI)** to enhance the user experience. The **Galaxy S25 Ultra** takes full advantage of **AI technology**, integrating it across various functions, from **camera optimization** to **battery management** and even **user interface customization**. Samsung's use of AI enables a smarter, more personalized experience that learns from your habits and preferences, offering tailored suggestions and automating tasks to save time and effort.

5. The 5000mAh Battery and Fast Charging Technology
As smartphones have become more powerful, the demand for longer battery life has also increased. Samsung responded to this need with the **5000mAh battery** in the **Galaxy S25 Ultra**, offering users the ability to power through their day without worrying about charging.

Alongside the larger battery, the **S25 Ultra** also supports **45W wired charging** and **15W wireless charging**, ensuring that the phone can be quickly powered up when needed.

6. Titanium Frame and Gorilla Armor Glass
One of the most striking features of the **Samsung Galaxy S25 Ultra** is its **titanium frame** and **Gorilla Armor 2 glass**, making the device incredibly durable while maintaining its premium aesthetic. This combination of durability and elegance represents Samsung's commitment to providing a long-lasting and visually appealing product that can withstand the rigors of daily life.

These milestones, along with countless other refinements in design, performance, and software, have culminated in the creation of the **Galaxy S25 Ultra**. This smartphone is the embodiment of Samsung's relentless pursuit of excellence, representing the next step in the evolution of the Galaxy S lineup.

CHAPTER 3

Unveiling the Galaxy S25 Ultra

The **Samsung Galaxy S25 Ultra** is not just another smartphone; it is the culmination of years of innovation and design excellence. Samsung has established itself as a leader in the smartphone industry by consistently pushing the boundaries of technology, and the **Galaxy S25 Ultra** is a testament to that commitment. This chapter delves into the official announcement and release of the **Samsung Galaxy S25 Ultra**, the design philosophy behind it, and the key features and specifications that make it one of the most advanced smartphones on the market today.

3.1 Announcement and Release

On **January 22, 2025**, Samsung made waves in the tech world by officially unveiling the **Galaxy S25 Ultra** during its highly anticipated **Samsung Unpacked event**. This event, streamed live to millions of viewers worldwide, marked the official introduction of Samsung's flagship smartphone for the year. As expected from Samsung, the **S25 Ultra** was presented as the brand's most innovative device to date, featuring the latest advancements in mobile technology, all packed into a sleek, premium design.

The **announcement** of the Galaxy S25 Ultra was met with excitement and anticipation, not only from Samsung's loyal customer base but also from tech enthusiasts, industry professionals, and critics. Samsung's Unpacked events have always been a momentous occasion, and the unveiling of the **S25 Ultra** was no exception. The event highlighted the device's premium build quality, cutting-edge camera system, and impressive software features.

What made the announcement even more exciting was the promise of a **revolutionary mobile experience**, powered by **AI technologies**, **5G connectivity**, and **future-proof hardware**. The **S25 Ultra** was positioned as a smartphone that could handle everything, from casual use to professional tasks, all while delivering an exceptional user experience. It was clear that this device was more than just a phone—it was a powerful tool designed for users who demand the best of everything: performance, design, and functionality.

In addition to the announcement, Samsung provided details on the **release date** of the Galaxy S25 Ultra. Pre-orders for the device began shortly after the event, with the official release scheduled for **February 7, 2025**. This release date generated even more buzz, as people around the world eagerly anticipated getting their hands on the latest flagship device. The Galaxy S25 Ultra was made available in a range of countries, with different pricing tiers based on storage options, ensuring that Samsung's latest creation was accessible to a wide range of consumers.

Samsung's announcement and release of the **Galaxy S25 Ultra** were followed by extensive marketing campaigns, which highlighted the device's standout features. Television commercials, online ads, and social media promotions helped to solidify the **S25 Ultra's** position as one of the most highly anticipated smartphones of the year. Samsung knew that this device would be pivotal in maintaining its position at the forefront of the smartphone industry, and the buzz surrounding the **S25 Ultra** only confirmed that the company had succeeded in creating something extraordinary.

3.2 Design Philosophy and Innovations

The **design philosophy** behind the **Samsung Galaxy S25 Ultra** is rooted in Samsung's long-standing tradition of combining **aesthetic appeal** with **practical functionality**. The device's design is a perfect balance of **sophistication, durability, and user experience**, incorporating the latest materials and technologies to create a smartphone that is not only visually striking but also highly functional.

Premium Materials and Durability

One of the most noticeable aspects of the **Galaxy S25 Ultra** is its premium **build quality**. The device features a **titanium frame**, which is a first for the Galaxy S series. This upgrade from aluminum to titanium makes the device stronger, more durable, and more resistant to scratches and drops. Titanium is known for its **lightweight properties** and its ability to withstand **impact** better than other metals, providing the **S25 Ultra** with a level of toughness that's unmatched by previous models.

On the front and back, the **Galaxy S25 Ultra** is protected by **Gorilla Armor 2 glass**, which offers enhanced protection against scratches, drops, and other everyday wear and tear. The combination of the titanium frame and Gorilla Armor glass not only makes the phone durable but also ensures that it maintains its sleek, premium appearance even after extended use.

Aesthetic Appeal and Ergonomics

Samsung has always placed a significant emphasis on **design aesthetics**, and the **S25 Ultra** is no exception. The device features a **sleek, modern design** with flat sides and gently rounded edges. This design choice helps to make the phone feel comfortable in the hand while also adding to its visual appeal. The **flat edges** of the device are a departure from the curved edges seen in earlier Galaxy S models, which were often criticized for being too prone to accidental touches. The flat sides make the **S25 Ultra** feel more balanced and secure, especially when using it with one hand.

In terms of **color options**, the **Galaxy S25 Ultra** comes in a range of sophisticated finishes, including **Titanium Silverblue**, **Titanium Black**, and **Titanium Gray**, each one giving the device a premium, polished look. There are also **exclusive online colors**, such as **Titanium Jetblack**, **Titanium Jadegreen**, and **Titanium Pinkgold**, which are available only through Samsung's official website. These options allow users to personalize their devices, ensuring that the **S25 Ultra** reflects their unique style.

The **ergonomics** of the device are also worth noting. The phone is designed to be **thin**, **light**, and **comfortable** to hold, with no sharp corners or edges that could cause discomfort. Whether you're holding the device for extended periods or using it in one hand, the **S25 Ultra** feels incredibly **ergonomic** and easy to use, making it suitable for both casual users and those who require the phone for professional tasks.

Display Innovation: The Infinity Display

A signature feature of Samsung smartphones has always been their **displays**, and the **S25 Ultra** continues this tradition with its **6.9-inch Dynamic LTPO AMOLED 2X** screen. The **Infinity Display**, which stretches from edge to edge, provides users with an immersive visual experience, perfect for everything from watching movies and gaming to browsing the web and multitasking.

The display is **stunningly vibrant** with a **3120x1440 pixel resolution**, ensuring that every image, video, and text looks incredibly sharp and lifelike. The **120Hz refresh rate** provides smooth scrolling, reducing motion blur and improving the overall responsiveness of the device. Additionally, the **LTPO (Low-Temperature Polycrystalline Oxide)** technology allows the screen to adapt to different refresh rates, depending on the content being displayed. This feature helps to **optimize battery life**, ensuring that the device can run for longer periods without sacrificing performance.

The **S25 Ultra's** display is also **HDR10+ certified**, ensuring that content with high dynamic range is displayed with enhanced contrast, brightness, and color accuracy. Whether you're watching a movie in **4K resolution** or playing the latest mobile games, the **S25 Ultra's display** offers an exceptional visual experience that rivals other premium smartphones on the market.

3.3 Key Features and Specifications

The **Samsung Galaxy S25 Ultra** is packed with **cutting-edge technology** and features that elevate it above other smartphones. From its **powerful performance** to its **innovative camera system**, the S25 Ultra is designed to meet the needs of users who demand the best in all areas.

Performance and Hardware

At the heart of the **S25 Ultra** is the **Qualcomm Snapdragon 8 Elite** processor, which is a significant leap forward in terms of **performance** and **efficiency**. The **Snapdragon 8 Elite** offers a **37% boost in CPU performance**, a **30% improvement in GPU capabilities**, and a **40% increase in AI processing power** compared to its predecessor. This powerful chipset ensures that the **S25 Ultra** can handle even the most demanding tasks, including **gaming**, **multitasking**, and **video editing**.

The **S25 Ultra** is equipped with **12GB of RAM** as standard, ensuring smooth multitasking and fast app switching. For storage, the device offers **256GB**, **512GB**, and **1TB** options, giving users plenty of space to store their apps, photos, videos, and other data. With **5G connectivity**, the **S25 Ultra** supports ultra-fast data speeds, ensuring that users can stream content, download files, and play online games with minimal lag or buffering.

Camera System

One of the standout features of the **S25 Ultra** is its **camera system**, which is the most advanced Samsung has ever put into a smartphone. The **200MP wide-angle lens** offers incredibly high-resolution photos with exceptional detail, while the **50MP ultra-wide lens** allows users to capture expansive landscapes or fit more into their shots. The **10MP periscope telephoto lens** offers **5x optical zoom**, making it possible to take stunning close-up shots without sacrificing image quality.

The **S25 Ultra's** camera system is also enhanced by **AI-powered features**, which help improve image quality in a variety of scenarios. Whether you're shooting in low light, capturing fast-moving objects, or recording video, the **AI system** adjusts settings automatically to ensure optimal results. The device also offers **8K video recording**, allowing users to capture **incredibly high-quality footage**.

Battery and Charging

With a **5000mAh battery**, the **S25 Ultra** offers **all-day battery life**, even with heavy use. The phone supports **45W wired charging**, allowing users to charge the device quickly and get back to using it. **15W wireless charging** is also supported, providing convenient charging options for users who prefer to go wire-free. The **S25 Ultra** also features **reverse wireless charging**, allowing users to charge other devices, such as wireless earbuds or smartwatches, directly from the phone.

Software and AI Integration

The **S25 Ultra** runs on **Android 15** with **One UI 7**, Samsung's custom skin that provides an intuitive and user-friendly interface. **Galaxy AI** plays a significant role in the software experience, allowing the device to learn from user behavior and provide personalized recommendations, automate tasks, and optimize performance. The **S25 Ultra** is also equipped with advanced security features, such as **facial recognition** and an **ultrasonic fingerprint scanner**, ensuring that user data remains secure.

The **Samsung Galaxy S25 Ultra** is a technological marvel that pushes the boundaries of what a smartphone can do. With its stunning design, powerful performance, cutting-edge camera system, and AI-powered features, the **S25**

Ultra is built to meet the needs of today's mobile users. Whether you're a professional, a photographer, a gamer, or simply someone who appreciates the best in mobile technology, the **S25 Ultra** offers an experience that is unmatched by other devices on the market.

CHAPTER 4

Design and Build Quality

The **Samsung Galaxy S25 Ultra** is not just a smartphone; it is a masterclass in design and build quality. Every inch of the device has been crafted with attention to detail, offering a blend of durability, functionality, and visual appeal. In this chapter, we will delve into the **materials and durability** that make the Galaxy S25 Ultra stand out, the **display enhancements** that elevate the viewing experience, and the **ergonomics and user experience** that ensure the device is comfortable and easy to use.

4.1 Materials and Durability

Samsung's design philosophy for the **Galaxy S25 Ultra** focuses on using **premium materials** that enhance both the aesthetic and functional qualities of the device. In terms of **build quality**, the **S25 Ultra** sets a new standard in the smartphone industry, combining **advanced materials** for both **strength** and **luxury**. Samsung has chosen to use the **highest-quality components** to ensure that this flagship device offers exceptional durability while maintaining its sleek and modern design.

Titanium Frame: Strength and Lightness Combined

One of the most significant updates to the design of the **Galaxy S25 Ultra** is the introduction of a **titanium frame**. This is a significant departure from the aluminum frames used in earlier Galaxy S models, providing a stronger, more resilient structure. Titanium is renowned for its strength, **lightweight** properties, and **resistance to corrosion**, making it the ideal material for a flagship device that is meant to withstand the rigors of daily use.

The **titanium frame** is not only durable but also adds a premium feel to the device. Its **lightweight nature** ensures that the phone remains easy to handle and doesn't feel cumbersome despite its large size. Moreover, titanium has a natural resistance to scratching, meaning the frame will stay looking pristine over time, even with regular handling. It is one of the **sturdiest materials** available for smartphone frames, providing **extra protection** against drops and other impacts. This durability is a critical feature for users who want a phone that will last for years without showing signs of wear and tear.

Gorilla Armor 2 Glass: The Ultimate Protection

Another key material used in the construction of the **Samsung Galaxy S25 Ultra** is **Gorilla Armor 2 glass**, which covers both the front and back of the device. This specially engineered glass offers unparalleled **resistance to scratches, shattering**, and **fingerprint smudges**, ensuring that the device remains in excellent condition even after prolonged use.

Gorilla Armor 2 glass is designed to be incredibly tough while maintaining a sleek, polished finish. It is resistant to both **scratches** from sharp objects and **cracks** caused by drops or impacts, providing an added layer of protection for the device. The glass also has a **smudge-resistant coating**, which helps keep the phone clean and fingerprint-free, ensuring that it always looks immaculate.

Not only does Gorilla Armor 2 provide **toughness**, but it also enhances the **visual clarity** and **vibrancy** of the display, ensuring that the viewing experience remains crisp and vibrant without the distracting effect of smudges or scratches. The glass is designed to work harmoniously with the device's **Dynamic LTPO AMOLED 2X** display, allowing users to enjoy the phone's stunning visuals without sacrificing durability.

IP68 Rating: Dust and Water Resistance

The **Samsung Galaxy S25 Ultra** is **IP68 certified**, meaning it is both **dustproof** and **water-resistant**. This certification ensures that the phone is fully protected from dust, dirt, and other small particles that could compromise its functionality. Additionally, the phone can withstand submersion in **up to 1.5 meters of water** for **30 minutes**, making it more resistant to accidental spills, rain, or submersions in water.

This **water resistance** adds a level of convenience for users who are often on the go. Whether you're caught in a sudden rainstorm or accidentally drop your phone into a pool, you can rest assured that the **S25 Ultra** is built to handle the situation with ease. The **IP68 rating** makes this device a reliable companion for those who want a smartphone that can withstand the elements without compromising on performance.

Scratch-Resistant and Impact-Proof Design

In addition to the **titanium frame** and **Gorilla Armor 2 glass**, the **S25 Ultra's** design features a reinforced structure that makes the device **resistant to scratches** and **impacts**. The **precise construction** of the phone's components ensures that the device feels solid and durable, even under heavy use. Whether you're placing the phone in your pocket, using it with a case, or carrying it around in your bag, you can trust that the **Galaxy S25 Ultra** is built to withstand the wear and tear of daily life.

4.2 Display Enhancements

The **display** is arguably one of the most important features of any smartphone, and the **Samsung Galaxy S25 Ultra** does not disappoint in this department. The phone's **6.9-inch Dynamic LTPO AMOLED 2X** display is a **visual masterpiece** that takes full advantage of Samsung's innovative screen technology. In this section, we will explore the key **display enhancements** that make the **S25 Ultra** a standout device in terms of visual quality, including its **vibrant colors**, **high resolution**, and **advanced refresh rate**.

Superb Color Accuracy and Brightness

The **S25 Ultra's Dynamic LTPO AMOLED 2X** display offers one of the most **vivid, true-to-life color experiences** available on a smartphone. The screen supports **HDR10+**, ensuring that users can enjoy **high dynamic range** content with **enhanced contrast**, **brighter whites**, and **deeper blacks**. The display has been calibrated to deliver the **most accurate colors** possible, which is especially important for users who enjoy watching movies or editing photos and videos on their devices.

The **S25 Ultra's screen** is also **incredibly bright**, with a peak brightness of **1,500 nits**, making it easy to view the screen even in bright sunlight or outdoor environments. This high level of brightness ensures that the phone remains usable in a wide range of lighting conditions, from dimly lit rooms to bright, sunny days.

High Resolution and Pixel Density

With a **3120x1440 pixel resolution** and an astonishing **511 pixels per inch (PPI)**, the **S25 Ultra** offers an ultra-high-definition viewing experience. The sharpness and clarity of the screen are second to none, making every image, video, and piece of text appear **incredibly crisp** and **detailed**. Whether you're browsing the web, watching high-definition content, or playing mobile games, the display ensures that every visual element looks **lifelike** and **immersive**.

120Hz Adaptive Refresh Rate

One of the most exciting features of the **S25 Ultra's display** is its **120Hz adaptive refresh rate**. This means that the screen can refresh up to **120 times per second**, resulting in **exceptionally smooth animations**, **scrolling**, and **gaming performance**. Whether you're browsing through social media feeds, scrolling through websites, or playing the latest mobile games, the **120Hz refresh rate** ensures that every interaction feels fluid and responsive.

The **adaptive** nature of the refresh rate means that the display can adjust its refresh rate based on the content being displayed. For example, when watching static content like photos or reading text, the refresh rate can lower to save battery life, while interactive content like games or videos will benefit from the high refresh rate for smoother motion. This balance between performance and energy efficiency ensures that the **S25 Ultra's** display delivers the best of both worlds.

Edge Display and Immersive Experience

The **S25 Ultra** continues the tradition of offering an **edge-to-edge display**, maximizing the screen real estate and minimizing bezels for an immersive viewing experience. The **Infinity Display** design stretches from one side of the device to the other, creating an **almost bezel-less effect**. This makes the **S25 Ultra** ideal for watching videos, playing games, or even multitasking, as the expansive screen offers more room for content and productivity.

In addition to the expansive screen, the **S25 Ultra's** edge display enhances functionality by allowing users to access apps, shortcuts, and notifications with ease. Samsung's **One UI** software integrates seamlessly with the edge display, offering features like **Edge Panels** that provide quick access to frequently used apps, contacts, and tools. This **innovative design** makes the **S25 Ultra** not only beautiful but also incredibly functional.

4.3 Ergonomics and User Experience

While the **design and durability** of a smartphone are critical, how it feels in your hand and how comfortable it is to use are equally important. The **Samsung Galaxy S25 Ultra** excels in this regard, offering a user experience that combines **comfort**, **efficiency**, and **ease of use**. In this section, we will explore the **ergonomics** of the device and how Samsung has optimized the **user experience** for maximum satisfaction.

Comfortable Grip and One-Handed Use

Despite its large **6.9-inch display**, the **S25 Ultra** is designed to be **comfortable to hold** and use. The phone's slim profile and **rounded edges** ensure that it fits comfortably in the hand, and the **flat sides** of the device provide a secure grip. Samsung has paid close attention to the **ergonomics** of the device, ensuring that it feels **natural** to hold and use for extended periods of time.

For users who prefer to operate their smartphone with one hand, the **S25 Ultra** is still manageable. The slightly curved edges and **slim design** allow the phone to fit well in the palm, and the **One UI** software includes features like **one-handed mode**, which reduces the screen size for easier access to all areas of the display with just one hand. This attention to detail makes the **S25 Ultra** not only a **premium** device but also a **practical** one.

Customization and Software Features

Samsung's **One UI 7**, built on **Android 15**, enhances the **user experience** by offering intuitive software features and customization options. The interface is designed to be user-friendly, with large icons and simplified navigation that make it easy to find and use the apps and features you need. The **S25 Ultra's** software integrates well with the hardware, offering smooth transitions, easy multitasking, and customization options that allow users to personalize their device to fit their preferences.

Samsung's commitment to **software refinement** ensures that the **S25 Ultra** provides an experience that is not only functional but also enjoyable. Features like **Edge Panels**, **split-screen multitasking**, and **AI-based enhancements** make the device more intuitive, allowing users to get the most out of their device with minimal effort.

Long-Term Comfort and User Satisfaction

The **Samsung Galaxy S25 Ultra** is designed for users who spend long hours on their devices. The **smooth performance**, **comfortable grip**, and **optimized software** ensure that the device is pleasant to use throughout the day. Whether you're watching a movie, playing a game, or working on a project, the **S25 Ultra** provides a **comfortable** and **efficient** user experience.

The **Samsung Galaxy S25 Ultra** is a marvel of design, combining **premium materials**, **advanced display technology**, and **thoughtful ergonomics** to create a device that is not only durable but also a joy to use. From its **titanium frame** and **Gorilla Armor 2 glass** to its **stunning display** and **comfortable handling**, the **S25 Ultra** offers an experience that balances **form** and **function** seamlessly. Whether you're a casual user or a tech enthusiast, the **S25 Ultra** provides a smartphone experience that is both **cutting-edge** and **user-friendly**.

CHAPTER 5

Performance and Hardware

The **Samsung Galaxy S25 Ultra** is not just a premium device in terms of design and features, it is also a powerhouse when it comes to performance and hardware. The performance of a smartphone is primarily defined by its **processor, RAM, storage, battery life**, and **charging capabilities**—and in these areas, the **S25 Ultra** excels. From running demanding applications and games to providing long-lasting battery life, the **S25 Ultra** is engineered to provide a smooth, seamless experience no matter the task at hand. This chapter will dive deep into the key components that contribute to the performance of the **S25 Ultra**, including the **processor and RAM, storage options**, and **battery life and charging capabilities**.

5.1 Processor and RAM

The heart of any high-performance smartphone is its **processor**, and the **Samsung Galaxy S25 Ultra** is powered by the **Qualcomm Snapdragon 8 Elite**, one of the most powerful processors in the market today. This cutting-edge chipset is designed to handle everything from gaming to multitasking with ease, offering impressive performance and efficiency that ensures smooth operation for all types of applications and activities. The **Snapdragon 8 Elite** represents a significant step forward in mobile processing, offering a range of improvements over its predecessors.

Snapdragon 8 Elite: The Powerhouse Behind the S25 Ultra

The **Snapdragon 8 Elite** is the latest in Qualcomm's line of flagship mobile processors, and it provides substantial performance improvements compared to previous generations. One of the most notable improvements is its **CPU** capabilities. The **Snapdragon 8 Elite** boasts a **37% improvement in CPU performance**, meaning that tasks requiring processing power—such as video editing, 3D rendering, and gaming—can be executed with ease. This results in faster app loading times, quicker multitasking, and overall smoother operation.

In addition to CPU improvements, the **Snapdragon 8 Elite** offers a **30% boost in GPU performance**. The **Adreno 740 GPU** in the **S25 Ultra** allows for enhanced graphics performance, ensuring that high-end games and graphical applications run without lag or stuttering. Whether you're playing the latest mobile games or viewing ultra-high-definition content, the **Adreno 740 GPU** ensures a visually immersive experience.

Another key aspect of the **Snapdragon 8 Elite** is its **AI capabilities**. With a **40% improvement in AI processing power**, the **S25 Ultra** can handle complex tasks that require machine learning and artificial intelligence, such as image recognition, voice assistance, and real-time translations. The integration of AI also helps with optimizing battery life, managing memory, and improving the camera system, which is powered by AI-driven enhancements for better low-light performance and subject tracking.

12GB RAM: Multitasking Made Effortless

When it comes to **RAM**, the **Samsung Galaxy S25 Ultra** comes equipped with a generous **12GB of RAM** as standard. This level of memory ensures that the device can easily handle a multitude of apps running simultaneously without slowing down. Whether you're switching between multiple browser tabs, using productivity apps, or playing demanding games, the **S25 Ultra** delivers a smooth and responsive experience.

For power users who enjoy running several apps at once, **12GB of RAM** provides more than enough headroom. Users can switch between apps with little to no delay, and large files can be handled quickly without causing the system to stutter or freeze. In addition to the large amount of RAM, the

S25 Ultra also features **advanced memory management software**, which ensures that the phone is always running at peak efficiency. Apps and data that are not being actively used are intelligently placed in a low-power state to save energy while still being ready for quick access when needed.

Future-Proof Performance

The combination of the **Snapdragon 8 Elite** and **12GB of RAM** ensures that the **Samsung Galaxy S25 Ultra** is **future-proof**. This means that the device will continue to perform well for years to come, even as apps and games become more demanding. Whether you're running the latest version of a productivity app or enjoying next-generation mobile games, the **S25 Ultra** offers the processing power necessary to handle all of your tasks with ease.

5.2 Storage Options

When it comes to **storage**, the **Galaxy S25 Ultra** offers a wide range of options to cater to the different needs of consumers. Whether you're someone who uses their phone to store large amounts of data or someone who prefers cloud-based storage, Samsung has ensured that the **S25 Ultra** is equipped with ample storage space and fast storage technologies to accommodate various use cases.

256GB, 512GB, and 1TB Storage Options

The **Galaxy S25 Ultra** is available in **three storage variants**: **256GB**, **512GB**, and **1TB**. These options provide plenty of room for users to store apps, photos, videos, and other data without running into storage limitations. For users who frequently download large files, install numerous apps, or store a large media library, the **1TB model** offers a massive amount of storage space, ensuring that you won't need to worry about running out of room anytime soon.

The **512GB** and **256GB** models provide plenty of storage for most users, offering a balanced solution for those who need substantial space but don't require the **1TB option**. Whether you're a **casual user** who mainly uses their phone for social media and messaging or a **power user** who needs space for extensive media libraries and professional files, the **S25 Ultra**'s storage options cater to every need.

UFS 4.0 Storage: Faster Than Ever

The **S25 Ultra** features the **UFS 4.0 storage standard**, which offers substantial improvements over previous generations in terms of **speed** and **efficiency**. With **UFS 4.0**, users can expect faster read and write speeds, meaning that the device can load apps, transfer files, and process data significantly faster than earlier models. The **S25 Ultra**'s

UFS 4.0 storage also contributes to its overall **performance** by allowing for quicker access to large files, resulting in an overall smoother user experience.

For users who are transferring large amounts of data, editing videos, or working with high-resolution images, the faster storage speeds provided by **UFS 4.0** make tasks quicker and more efficient. This technology ensures that the phone remains responsive, even when handling large files and demanding apps.

No Expandable Storage

One downside to the **S25 Ultra** is the absence of a **microSD card slot** for expandable storage, which is a feature found on many previous Samsung smartphones. While this may be a limitation for some users who prefer to expand their storage capacity, Samsung has compensated by offering the device in multiple large storage options, including the massive **1TB version**. For most users, the available storage should be more than sufficient, but those who require additional space for high-resolution media or large files will need to consider the model with more built-in storage.

Cloud Integration

While the **S25 Ultra** does not feature expandable storage, Samsung has integrated robust **cloud-based storage** options into the device. The **Samsung Cloud** and **Google Drive** offer seamless cloud storage solutions, allowing users to store files and media off-device without needing to worry about running out of storage space. With **5G connectivity**, uploading and downloading files to and from the cloud is incredibly fast, ensuring that users can access their data from anywhere at any time.

5.3 Battery Life and Charging Capabilities

Battery life is one of the most important considerations when choosing a smartphone. With the **Samsung Galaxy S25 Ultra**, Samsung has equipped the device with a **massive 5000mAh battery**, designed to ensure that the phone lasts all day on a single charge, even with demanding use. But the **S25 Ultra** doesn't just deliver exceptional battery life; it also offers **fast charging** and **advanced power management** features, making it one of the most power-efficient smartphones on the market.

5000mAh Battery: All-Day Usage

The **5000mAh battery** in the **S25 Ultra** provides a **long-lasting** power source, ensuring that users can enjoy a full day of use without needing to charge the phone. Whether you're using the phone for **productivity**, **entertainment**, **gaming**, or **communication**, the battery is designed to handle a full day's worth of activity without running out of power. Samsung has also optimized the device's **software** to ensure that power consumption is minimized when the device is idle or not in active use, extending battery life even further.

For users who tend to use their smartphones heavily throughout the day—whether for business calls, video streaming, or gaming—the **5000mAh battery** ensures that the **S25 Ultra** can keep up with demanding tasks. Even with intensive usage, the phone will continue to perform efficiently, without the need for frequent charging.

45W Wired Charging

One of the standout features of the **Galaxy S25 Ultra** is its support for **45W wired charging**. With **45W charging**, the **S25 Ultra** can be charged from **0% to 50% in just 20 minutes**, making it one of the fastest charging smartphones on the market. This feature is incredibly convenient for users who are in a hurry and need to quickly power up their device before heading out the door. Whether you're at home, at work, or on the go, the **45W wired charging** ensures that your device is ready to go in no time.

While the **45W charger** is sold separately, it is available for purchase through Samsung's official website and retail partners. For those who don't need to charge their device as quickly, **25W and 15W chargers** are also supported, offering flexibility depending on your needs and charging environment.

15W Wireless Charging and Reverse Wireless Charging

For users who prefer wireless charging, the **Galaxy S25 Ultra** supports **15W wireless charging**. This means that the phone can be charged wirelessly at a faster rate than many other smartphones on the market. The **15W wireless charging** is compatible with **Qi-certified wireless chargers**, ensuring that users can charge their device at home, in the office, or in the car with ease.

In addition to standard wireless charging, the **S25 Ultra** also supports **reverse wireless charging**, allowing users to charge other devices, such as **wireless earbuds**, **smartwatches**, or even other smartphones, directly from the **S25 Ultra**. This feature is incredibly convenient for users who need to charge multiple devices while on the go, ensuring that your other devices remain powered throughout the day.

Battery Optimization and AI-Based Power Management

To complement the impressive hardware, Samsung has integrated **AI-powered battery optimization** features into the **S25 Ultra**. The phone intelligently learns from your usage patterns and adjusts power consumption accordingly, ensuring that you get the most out of the **5000mAh battery**. Whether you're using the phone for light tasks like browsing social media or more power-hungry activities like gaming, the phone adapts to ensure that power is used efficiently.

Features like **adaptive brightness**, **background app management**, and **power-saving modes** help ensure that the **S25 Ultra** lasts as long as possible throughout the day. The AI also helps monitor power-hungry apps and processes, making adjustments as needed to optimize battery performance.

The **Samsung Galaxy S25 Ultra** delivers impressive performance and hardware, ensuring that users have the power they need for any task. With its **Snapdragon 8 Elite processor**, **12GB of RAM**, and **generous storage options**, the **S25 Ultra** is designed to handle demanding applications, multitasking, and high-end gaming with ease. The **5000mAh battery**, combined with **45W wired charging** and **15W wireless charging**, ensures that the device will last all day and recharge quickly when needed. With **AI-powered**

optimization and cutting-edge storage technology, the **S25 Ultra** offers a seamless and efficient experience that can meet the needs of the most demanding users. Whether you're looking for a high-performance phone for work, entertainment, or gaming, the **S25 Ultra** delivers in every aspect.

CHAPTER 6

Camera Capabilities

The **Samsung Galaxy S25 Ultra** stands out as one of the most impressive smartphones for photography and videography, thanks to its cutting-edge camera technology. Whether you're capturing breathtaking landscapes, shooting professional-level videos, or simply snapping everyday photos, the **S25 Ultra's** camera system offers remarkable quality. In this chapter, we'll explore the **camera hardware**, **software enhancements**, and the **real-world performance** of the camera system, giving you an in-depth understanding of how the **Galaxy S25 Ultra** excels in the world of mobile photography.

6.1 Camera Hardware Overview

At the heart of the **Samsung Galaxy S25 Ultra**'s camera system is a **multi-lens array** that offers versatility, exceptional detail, and the ability to capture high-quality images across a wide range of shooting conditions. The **S25 Ultra** features a robust camera setup that combines **high-resolution sensors**, advanced **zoom capabilities**, and **specialized lenses** to provide users with professional-grade photography and videography.

200MP Wide-Angle Lens

The flagship camera on the **Galaxy S25 Ultra is its 200MP wide-angle sensor**, which is the highest resolution sensor ever used in a Samsung Galaxy smartphone. This cutting-edge sensor offers immense detail and clarity, allowing users to capture stunning, high-resolution images with remarkable depth. The **200MP camera** uses a combination of **pixel binning** technology, which merges smaller pixels into larger ones to improve light sensitivity and dynamic range, resulting in sharp, bright, and detailed images.

This lens is perfect for shooting landscapes, architecture, or any scene where fine details matter. With **200MP**, you can crop into your images without sacrificing quality, enabling you to zoom in and extract details that would otherwise be lost with lower-resolution sensors.

50MP Ultra-Wide Lens

The **50MP ultra-wide lens** is designed for capturing expansive scenes, such as group photos, sweeping landscapes, and architectural shots. Offering a **120-degree field of view**, the **ultra-wide lens** allows users to fit more into the frame without needing to step back. This lens is an essential tool for anyone who needs to capture more of a scene in a single shot, whether it's a cityscape or a wide group photo.

The **50MP resolution** ensures that even wide-angle shots are sharp and clear, with less distortion at the edges compared to other wide-angle lenses. This makes it ideal for professional-level work, where image quality is paramount even in wide-field photography.

10MP Periscope Telephoto Lens with 5x Optical Zoom

The **10MP periscope telephoto lens** with **5x optical zoom** offers incredible versatility when it comes to shooting distant subjects without losing image quality. **Optical zoom** allows users to zoom in without sacrificing clarity, ensuring that even distant subjects remain sharp and well-defined. Whether you're capturing wildlife from a distance, shooting sports action, or snapping close-up shots of architectural details, the **periscope telephoto lens** ensures that your subject stays crisp and clear, even at long distances.

This lens also excels in low-light conditions, where it uses **advanced optical stabilization** to reduce blur and ensure sharp images, even when shooting handheld.

12MP Front-Facing Camera

For selfies and video calls, the **S25 Ultra** is equipped with a **12MP front-facing camera**, which offers excellent performance in terms of both image quality and video recording. The **12MP sensor** delivers bright, clear selfies with accurate skin tones and vibrant colors, making it an ideal choice for social media enthusiasts and content creators. The camera also supports **4K video recording**, allowing users to capture high-quality video from the front-facing lens.

With **AI-powered enhancements**, the front camera also offers **portrait mode** for a soft, professional-looking background blur that highlights the subject in the foreground, giving selfies a more polished and cinematic feel.

Laser Autofocus and Dual Pixel Technology

The **S25 Ultra's camera system** incorporates **laser autofocus** and **dual-pixel autofocus technology**, which ensures quick and accurate focusing even in challenging conditions. Laser autofocus helps the camera lock onto subjects more quickly and accurately, especially in low-light or fast-moving scenarios. Dual-pixel technology further enhances autofocus by providing dual photodiodes on each pixel, improving the camera's ability to focus rapidly, ensuring sharpness and clarity in every shot.

Advanced Optical Image Stabilization (OIS)

To complement the camera's impressive lens array, the **S25 Ultra** incorporates **optical image stabilization (OIS)** to minimize motion blur caused by shaky hands during low-light or long-exposure shots. Whether you're shooting in **dimly lit environments** or capturing fast-moving subjects, **OIS** ensures that the images remain stable and clear, even when the camera is in motion.

6.2 Software Enhancements and Features

The **Samsung Galaxy S25 Ultra**'s camera hardware is complemented by a wide range of **software enhancements** that help to optimize image quality and provide users with greater creative control. Samsung has integrated **AI technologies**, **advanced software algorithms**, and **photographic modes** that make the **S25 Ultra**'s camera system both powerful and easy to use.

AI-Powered Scene Optimization

One of the most important software features of the **S25 Ultra** is **AI scene optimization**. This feature uses **machine learning** to analyze the subject of the image and automatically adjust settings such as **color balance**, **contrast**, **brightness**, and **sharpness** to optimize the shot. The **AI system** recognizes over 30 different types of scenes, including landscapes, food, portraits, and pets, ensuring that each shot is perfectly tuned for the subject you're photographing.

For example, when you take a photo of a sunset, the AI will automatically adjust the exposure to bring out the rich colors of the sky, while ensuring that the subject of the photo remains clear. In portrait shots, the AI will adjust the lighting to emphasize the subject's face and ensure the background remains blurred in a natural, appealing way.

Super Steady Video Recording

For videographers, the **S25 Ultra** offers **Super Steady video recording**, which is powered by both **optical image stabilization (OIS)** and **AI-based motion stabilization**. This feature helps eliminate shakes and jitters while filming, allowing you to record smooth, cinematic video footage, even when moving quickly or walking. This is particularly useful for action shots, travel videos, and vlogs, where stability is essential for maintaining a high-quality video.

Super Steady video also works in **4K** resolution, giving you the flexibility to record both smooth and detailed videos, even in challenging environments.

Night Mode and Low-Light Photography

The **S25 Ultra** excels in **low-light photography** thanks to its advanced **Night Mode** and **AI-enhanced low-light algorithms**. When shooting in dimly lit environments, the camera automatically switches to **Night Mode**, where it uses multiple exposures and combines them into a single, bright, and clear image. **AI** helps to improve details and reduce noise in dark scenes, so your photos look brighter and more detailed without overexposing lighter areas.

Whether you're capturing city lights at night, shooting indoors, or taking a portrait in low light, the **S25 Ultra's Night Mode** ensures that the camera produces clear, vibrant images with minimal noise.

Portrait Mode and Depth Control

Another important feature of the **S25 Ultra's camera** is its **portrait mode**, which uses advanced **depth sensing** to create professional-looking images with a soft, blurred background (known as **bokeh**) while keeping the subject in sharp focus. The **AI** algorithms not only detect the subject's face but also adjust lighting and focus to enhance the effect. Portrait shots appear as though they were taken with a professional DSLR camera, with the background artistically blurred to highlight the subject.

In addition to portrait mode, the **S25 Ultra** offers **depth control**, allowing users to adjust the intensity of the background blur after the photo has been taken, providing a **high level of creative control**.

Pro Mode and Manual Controls

For users who want to take complete control over their photography, the **S25 Ultra** includes a **Pro Mode**, which allows access to **manual controls** for settings such as **ISO**, **shutter speed**, **exposure**, and **white balance**. This mode is ideal for photographers who are familiar with manual photography techniques and want to experiment with different settings to capture the perfect shot.

The **Pro Mode** also supports **RAW image capture**, giving photographers uncompressed image files that preserve all the details and dynamic range. This is perfect for editing and post-processing, allowing users to make adjustments without losing image quality.

AI-Powered Video Editor

The **S25 Ultra**'s camera system is also complemented by an **AI-powered video editor** that automatically analyzes your footage and suggests edits to improve your video. It can detect the best moments from your footage, apply transitions, add music, and even stabilize shaky footage. This feature is great for vloggers, social media creators, and anyone who wants to create polished videos without needing to edit them manually.

6.3 Real-World Photography and Videography Performance

While the **specs** and **software enhancements** of the **S25 Ultra**'s camera system are impressive on paper, it's the real-world performance that truly showcases how well this device excels in photography and videography. In this section, we'll examine how the camera system performs in everyday scenarios, from casual snapshots to professional-level video recording.

Daylight Photography: Crisp, Vibrant Shots

During the day, the **200MP wide-angle sensor** captures **incredible detail**, with images that remain sharp even after cropping. Whether you're taking **landscape shots**, **street photography**, or **group portraits**, the **S25 Ultra** excels in producing **vivid colors** and **dynamic range**. The **AI optimization** ensures that photos appear natural, without over-saturating colors or introducing unnatural effects. Even challenging lighting situations, such as backlit scenes or harsh sunlight, are handled with ease, with the camera adjusting exposure automatically to ensure that subjects are properly illuminated.

For those who prefer to shoot in **manual mode**, the **S25 Ultra** offers extensive options for adjusting ISO, shutter speed, and white balance, giving you full creative control over the image. Whether you're an experienced photographer or just starting out, the camera system is designed to deliver high-quality results.

Low-Light and Night Photography: Exceptional Detail in the Dark

When the sun sets, the **S25 Ultra** continues to impress with its **low-light capabilities**. In **Night Mode**, the camera can capture incredibly bright and detailed images, even in near-complete darkness. Whether you're photographing a city skyline at night or snapping photos indoors in low light, the **S25 Ultra's** camera excels at **reducing noise** and retaining detail in shadows. The **AI** enhances the overall exposure, making the image appear more natural and avoiding overexposure in bright spots.

For users who like to get creative with night photography, the **S25 Ultra** also allows for **long-exposure shots**, which can be adjusted in **Pro Mode** for dynamic and artistic results.

Videography: Smooth, Professional-Level Recording

When it comes to videography, the **S25 Ultra** is equally impressive. The **Super Steady video feature** ensures that even handheld shots remain stable and smooth, making it perfect for **action shots**, **travel vlogs**, and **social media content**. **4K video recording** is available on both the front and rear cameras, allowing you to capture high-quality video with stunning detail.

For more cinematic effects, the **S25 Ultra** supports **8K video recording**, offering an unprecedented level of detail that rivals professional cameras. Whether you're shooting for **YouTube**, **Instagram**, or simply capturing memories, the **S25 Ultra** makes it easy to create high-quality videos with minimal effort.

The **Samsung Galaxy S25 Ultra**'s camera system is a **tour de force** of mobile photography and videography, blending cutting-edge hardware with powerful software features. With its **200MP wide-angle lens**, **50MP ultra-wide lens**, **10MP periscope telephoto lens**, and **12MP front-facing camera**, the **S25 Ultra** is designed to capture stunning images and videos in any scenario. Whether you're a professional photographer, content creator, or casual user, the **S25 Ultra** delivers **exceptional quality**, **advanced features**, and **creative flexibility** that make it one of the most powerful camera systems available in a smartphone today. From **AI-powered enhancements** to **Super Steady video recording**, the **S25 Ultra** ensures that every shot, whether it's a photo or video, is nothing short of spectacular.

CHAPTER 7

Software and User Interface

The **Samsung Galaxy S25 Ultra** is not just a physical marvel of design and hardware; it is also powered by one of the most advanced and user-friendly software ecosystems available on a smartphone. The software experience is one of the most important aspects of any device, as it dictates how users interact with the hardware and how effectively the device meets their needs. In this chapter, we will explore the software that powers the **S25 Ultra**, specifically **Android 15** and **One UI 7**, along with the integration of **AI features** that make the device smarter and more intuitive. Finally, we will delve into user feedback and experience, examining how the software and interface translate into real-world usage.

7.1 Introduction to Android 15 and One UI 7

The **Samsung Galaxy S25 Ultra** runs on **Android 15**, the latest version of Google's mobile operating system. Android 15 brings a host of new features and optimizations that improve everything from **performance** to **security**. However, Samsung's unique skin on Android, **One UI 7**, is where the magic really happens. **One UI** is Samsung's custom interface designed to enhance the Android experience, offering a more intuitive, clean, and customizable user interface that feels both elegant and practical.

What is One UI 7?

One UI 7 is the latest iteration of Samsung's custom Android skin. It continues Samsung's philosophy of making smartphones more **user-centric**, focusing on ease of use, efficiency, and visual appeal. **One UI 7** refines the elements introduced in previous versions, making subtle but impactful changes that improve the user experience. The goal of **One UI** is to provide a seamless and **intuitive interface** that enhances accessibility, navigation, and customization while retaining all the features and functionality that Android offers.

In **One UI 7**, Samsung has made **several refinements** to the interface that make it cleaner, more efficient, and better suited for large screens, like the one on the **S25 Ultra**. The design has been streamlined to reduce **visual clutter**, with **more organized menus** and settings. There's a focus on **ease of navigation** with **larger icons** and **increased spacing** that makes everything easier to access, even with one hand.

Key Features of One UI 7

One of the standout features of **One UI 7** is its ability to make multitasking more accessible. It includes **Split-Screen Mode**, **Pop-up View**, and **Edge Panels**, which allow users to run multiple apps simultaneously with ease. These features are especially useful for power users who need to juggle several tasks at once, such as responding to emails, checking the calendar, and watching videos without switching between apps.

One UI 7 also introduces a **revamped notification system** that allows users to quickly sort through their alerts and manage them with more precision. Samsung has also enhanced the **Dark Mode** feature, making it easier on the eyes, especially in low-light environments. The **Always On Display** has been improved as well, providing users with more information without needing to wake the phone.

A key feature in **One UI 7** is its **customizability**. Users can change the look and feel of the UI through **themes**, **icons**, and **wallpapers**. There's also a range of **widgets** available to add to the home screen, including those for news, weather, and social media updates. **One UI 7** allows you to personalize the device in a way that suits your preferences and style.

Android 15 Enhancements

Android 15, the operating system that underpins **One UI 7**, introduces some exciting new features that improve the overall functionality of the phone. One of the most notable improvements is **Performance Mode**, which optimizes the system's power usage and helps preserve battery life while maintaining optimal performance. Android 15 also introduces **enhanced security features**, including a **refined biometric authentication system**, which is faster and more reliable.

Another key addition is the **AI-powered notifications**. Android 15 uses machine learning to prioritize and categorize notifications, ensuring that the most important ones appear first, while less urgent ones can be accessed at your convenience. This makes the notification system smarter and more organized, reducing the amount of time spent sorting through alerts.

In terms of **performance**, Android 15 is designed to work seamlessly with modern hardware, such as the **Snapdragon 8 Elite** in the **S25 Ultra**. Android 15 provides better **resource management**, ensuring that the **S25 Ultra** performs at its best, even when running heavy applications or multitasking.

7.2 AI Features and Integrations

One of the defining features of the **Samsung Galaxy S25 Ultra** is its **AI capabilities**. The **S25 Ultra** incorporates several advanced AI features that enhance the overall user experience, making the device smarter, more intuitive, and more personalized. From **camera enhancements** to **performance optimization**, AI is integrated throughout the system to make the device more efficient and capable of anticipating user needs.

AI Camera Enhancements

The **camera system** of the **S25 Ultra** is heavily powered by **AI**, which contributes to the device's ability to capture stunning photos and videos in a wide range of conditions. The **AI Scene Optimizer** automatically detects the subject of a photo and adjusts the settings accordingly to ensure the best possible results. For example, when photographing food, the camera enhances colors and sharpness to make the photo appear vibrant and appealing. When photographing landscapes, the AI ensures that the entire scene, from the foreground to the background, is well-exposed.

The **AI** also assists with **low-light photography** by improving the clarity and brightness of images captured in dim environments. The **AI-powered Night Mode** helps users capture clearer photos in near-total darkness, making it one of the best low-light cameras available in a smartphone today.

AI in Performance Optimization

AI is also used to optimize the **performance** of the **S25 Ultra**. The **Qualcomm Snapdragon 8 Elite** chipset integrates **AI** to manage power and performance based on user habits. For instance, the **AI** monitors how frequently apps are used and can prioritize resources for apps that are used most often while reducing the power allocated to less frequently used apps. This results in more efficient **battery life**, as the **S25 Ultra** intelligently adjusts the use of its resources.

Moreover, **AI-based Adaptive Battery** learns which apps you use most often and prioritizes their background activity, ensuring that apps you use on a regular basis are always running smoothly. Conversely, apps that are used less often consume less battery power in the background, optimizing battery life without compromising performance.

Bixby: Samsung's Virtual Assistant

Samsung's virtual assistant, **Bixby**, plays a crucial role in enhancing the AI experience on the **S25 Ultra**. Bixby is deeply integrated into the device, offering a range of features such as **voice commands**, **smart home integration**, and **personalized suggestions**. With the **Bixby Routines** feature, the assistant learns your habits and customizes the user experience by suggesting actions based on your usage patterns. For example, if you typically use the **S25 Ultra** for video calls during lunch breaks, Bixby will suggest launching your video calling app at that time, streamlining your workflow.

Bixby can also help automate tasks, such as adjusting settings based on time of day or location. For example, when you get home from work, Bixby can automatically adjust your phone's **Wi-Fi settings**, **sound profile**, and even turn on your **smart lights** if connected to a **Samsung SmartThings** ecosystem. This level of **integration** makes the **S25 Ultra** a central hub in a **smart home environment**, all thanks to the power of **AI**.

AI-Based Personalization

The **S25 Ultra**'s **AI** capabilities extend beyond system performance and camera enhancements. The device uses **machine learning** to personalize the user interface based on individual usage patterns. This means that over time, the phone learns your preferences and tailors notifications, app placements, and even app suggestions to suit your habits. For example, the **S25 Ultra** might suggest apps that you use most frequently or offer shortcuts to apps based on your location or the time of day.

Moreover, **One UI 7** introduces **AI-driven suggestions** for **wallpapers**, **themes**, and **widgets**, which adapt to your lifestyle and the apps you use. As the device learns more about your preferences, it continually fine-tunes the interface to provide a more personalized experience. Whether you want your home screen organized a certain way, or prefer certain themes, the **S25 Ultra's AI** ensures that it remains customized to your needs.

7.3 User Feedback and Experience

The **user experience** (UX) plays a critical role in determining how well a device integrates into daily life, and the **Samsung Galaxy S25 Ultra** delivers a premium experience in this regard. **One UI 7** is specifically designed to make **Android 15** more intuitive and accessible, offering an interface that prioritizes ease of use and efficiency. But how do users feel about the overall experience? In this section, we'll take a deep dive into user feedback and explore how the software experience translates into real-world usage.

Interface Simplicity and Ease of Navigation

One of the most frequently praised aspects of the **S25 Ultra** is the **user-friendly interface** provided by **One UI 7**. Users appreciate the **clean layout** and **minimalist design** that make it easy to navigate through the phone's settings, apps, and features. The **larger icons**, **increased spacing**, and **optimized navigation menus** make it simple to access and manage the phone's functions, whether you are a tech-savvy user or someone who prefers a more straightforward approach.

The **One UI 7**'s intuitive interface means that users don't have to search through endless menus or settings to find what they need. Common features are easily accessible, and more advanced settings can be found with just a few taps. Additionally, the **Gesture Navigation** in **One UI 7** makes it easy for users to switch between apps, return to the home screen, or open the multitasking view, all with simple swipes and gestures.

Smooth and Responsive Performance

The **S25 Ultra** offers **exceptional performance**, and users have expressed high satisfaction with its **responsiveness and speed**. Thanks to the powerful combination of the **Snapdragon 8 Elite processor** and **12GB of RAM**, the phone handles **multitasking, gaming,** and **heavy applications** with ease. Apps open quickly, and switching between them is seamless. Users report that the phone feels fast and responsive, even when running demanding apps or large files.

In terms of gaming, the **S25 Ultra** has received particularly favorable feedback. The **Adreno 740 GPU** ensures that games run smoothly, with high-quality graphics, even for graphically demanding titles. The **120Hz refresh rate** also contributes to a smoother visual experience, particularly when playing fast-paced games where responsiveness is crucial.

Battery Life Satisfaction

Battery life is always a point of concern for smartphone users, and the **S25 Ultra** has generally received positive feedback in this regard. With its **5000mAh battery**, the device can easily last through a full day of typical use, including browsing, social media, video streaming, and light gaming. Users have noted that the phone doesn't need frequent charging, even with heavy usage, and the **AI-powered battery management** ensures that battery consumption is optimized throughout the day.

The fast-charging capabilities, including **45W wired charging** and **15W wireless charging**, have also been praised by users who appreciate being able to quickly recharge the phone during busy days.

Bixby and AI Personalization

Bixby, Samsung's virtual assistant, has received mixed reviews. Some users find it **useful and effective**, especially with the integration of **Bixby Routines**, which automatically adjusts settings based on user behavior. For example, the ability to automate tasks like adjusting **Wi-Fi settings** when you arrive home or activating **Do Not Disturb** during meetings is a convenience that many appreciate. However, some users feel that Bixby could still be improved in terms of understanding natural language and offering more refined responses. While it is a helpful tool for **smart home integration** and hands-free commands, there is still room for improvement in its **voice recognition** and **accuracy**.

Overall User Experience

Overall, the feedback from users of the **S25 Ultra** is overwhelmingly positive. The combination of **One UI 7** and **Android 15** creates a seamless, intuitive experience that appeals to both power users and those who prefer a more straightforward interface. With its **AI enhancements**, smooth performance, and customizable options, the **S25 Ultra** offers a premium user experience that can easily cater to a wide range of needs and preferences. Whether you are a **photographer**, **gamer**, or **professional**, the S25 Ultra provides a **smooth** and **highly enjoyable experience** across the board.

The **Samsung Galaxy S25 Ultra** excels in both **hardware** and **software**, providing users with an experience that is both powerful and intuitive. With **Android 15** and **One UI 7**, Samsung has created a polished and user-friendly interface that is optimized for performance, ease of use, and personalization. The integration of **AI features** further enhances the user experience, making the phone smarter and more adaptable to individual needs. Based on **user feedback**, the S25 Ultra has received high marks for its performance, design, and software features, ensuring it stands out as one of the best smartphones on the market today.

CHAPTER 8

Awards and Recognitions

The **Samsung Galaxy S25 Ultra** is not only one of the most advanced smartphones on the market today, but it has also garnered significant attention in the form of prestigious **industry awards**, **critical acclaim**, and **enthusiastic user testimonials**. These accolades are a testament to the incredible effort Samsung has put into designing and developing a device that is a true game-changer in the smartphone market. This chapter will explore the **awards and recognitions** received by the **S25 Ultra**, including accolades from the tech industry, the praise it has garnered from critics, and the feedback from users who have experienced the device firsthand.

8.1 Industry Awards

The **Samsung Galaxy S25 Ultra** has captured the attention of many in the tech world and beyond, earning a number of prestigious industry awards for its innovative design, cutting-edge technology, and overall performance. These awards are not only a reflection of Samsung's engineering prowess but also a recognition of how well the **S25 Ultra** addresses the needs and demands of consumers.

Best Smartphone of 2025 – Tech Innovation Awards

The **Samsung Galaxy S25 Ultra** was awarded **Best Smartphone of 2025** by the **Tech Innovation Awards**, an event that honors the most groundbreaking devices and technologies in the tech industry. This award was given to the **S25 Ultra** because of its **pioneering features, state-of-the-art performance**, and **game-changing camera system**. The judges were particularly impressed by the **200MP camera**, which sets a new standard for smartphone photography, as well as the device's **advanced AI capabilities, 5G connectivity**, and **sleek design**.

The **S25 Ultra's** powerful **Snapdragon 8 Elite** processor and **12GB of RAM** were highlighted as key factors in its outstanding **performance**, ensuring that the device can handle any task thrown at it, from multitasking and gaming to running demanding apps. The phone's **5000mAh battery** and **45W wired charging** were also noted as impressive features, allowing users to go through the day without constantly worrying about recharging.

In particular, the **camera system** was considered one of the standout features, with the **200MP wide-angle lens, 50MP ultra-wide lens**, and **10MP periscope telephoto lens** earning praise for their ability to capture stunning images in a variety of conditions. This recognition solidified the **S25 Ultra** as one of the most remarkable smartphones of the year.

Best Display Technology – Display Innovation Awards

The **S25 Ultra** also won the **Best Display Technology** award at the **Display Innovation Awards**, thanks to its **6.9-inch Dynamic LTPO AMOLED 2X display**. Samsung has long been known for its display technology, and the **S25 Ultra** continues this tradition with a screen that is vibrant, immersive, and ultra-responsive. The **120Hz refresh rate** and **1200 nits peak brightness** ensure that content looks vibrant, even under bright sunlight, while the **LTPO technology** allows for adaptive refresh rates that save battery life.

The **S25 Ultra's Infinity Display** was praised for its seamless integration into the body of the phone, offering users an edge-to-edge display that makes watching videos, playing games, and browsing the internet a visually stunning experience. The **HDR10+ support** adds depth and contrast to content, further elevating the device's display capabilities. Samsung's commitment to excellence in display technology has once again been recognized with this prestigious award.

Best Camera Technology – Mobile Photography Awards

Another notable industry recognition for the **Samsung Galaxy S25 Ultra** came in the form of the **Best Camera Technology** award at the **Mobile Photography Awards**. The **200MP camera system** that includes a **50MP ultra-wide lens** and a **10MP telephoto lens** with **5x optical zoom** was praised for its incredible ability to capture rich, detailed images across a range of lighting conditions. The **AI-powered camera enhancements** were also highlighted as a critical feature, allowing the device to deliver superior results even in challenging environments.

The **AI scene optimization, Super Steady video recording**, and **Night Mode** were recognized as standout features that have made the **S25 Ultra** one of the most advanced smartphones for mobile photography and videography. Whether users are shooting landscapes, portraits, or action shots, the **camera system** of the **S25 Ultra** offers exceptional versatility and performance.

Sustainability Leadership Award – Global Technology Awards

Samsung's commitment to **sustainability** has also been acknowledged, as the **S25 Ultra** won the **Sustainability Leadership Award** at the **Global Technology Awards**. This recognition was given in light of the **S25 Ultra's** efforts to reduce its environmental impact through various means, including **eco-friendly packaging, energy-efficient components**, and the use of **recyclable materials** in its construction. Samsung's push toward sustainability is an important step in ensuring that smartphones have a more positive environmental footprint.

The **S25 Ultra's reduced carbon emissions** and **responsible manufacturing practices** are part of Samsung's broader commitment to creating more **eco-conscious devices** that contribute to a more sustainable future. This award underscores the importance of **green technology** in today's world and celebrates Samsung's efforts to lead by example in the mobile tech industry.

8.2 Critical Acclaim

In addition to industry awards, the **Samsung Galaxy S25 Ultra** has received **critical acclaim** from some of the most respected voices in the tech and mobile review industry. Expert reviewers have lauded the **S25 Ultra** for its **premium build quality, innovative camera system**, and **unmatched performance**, which combine to create one of the most compelling smartphones available.

TechRadar: "A Monumental Leap Forward"

In their review, **TechRadar** called the **S25 Ultra** "a monumental leap forward in smartphone technology." The review praised the **200MP camera** as one of the most exciting features of the device, noting that it "delivers incredible detail and clarity, whether you're capturing landscapes, portraits, or fast-moving action." The review also highlighted the device's **AI-driven optimizations**, which improve both performance and photography.

"Samsung has outdone itself with the **S25 Ultra**," the review concluded. "It's an all-around powerhouse that sets the bar for future smartphones." TechRadar was particularly impressed with the **battery life**, **charging speeds**, and **screen quality**, noting that Samsung has managed to strike a perfect balance between performance, design, and functionality.

The Verge: "Samsung's Best Flagship Yet"

The Verge took a detailed look at the **S25 Ultra**, calling it "Samsung's best flagship yet." The review emphasized how the device manages to deliver **exceptional performance** with its **Snapdragon 8 Elite processor** and **12GB of RAM**, making it an ideal choice for **gamers** and **power users** alike. The **120Hz refresh rate** and **6.9-inch Dynamic LTPO AMOLED 2X display** were singled out as some of the **best**

display technologies available, providing vibrant and smooth visuals for all types of content.

When discussing the **camera**, The Verge's review highlighted the **S25 Ultra's ability to capture high-quality photos and videos** in a variety of environments. "From bright, sunny days to low-light scenarios, the **S25 Ultra's** camera adapts effortlessly, delivering stunning results in every shot."

The review concluded that the **S25 Ultra** is an exceptional device that "combines premium design, cutting-edge technology, and powerful performance, making it one of the most complete smartphones on the market today."

CNET: "The Ultimate All-in-One Device"

In its review, **CNET** described the **Samsung Galaxy S25 Ultra** as "the ultimate all-in-one device." The review praised the **camera system**, noting that "Samsung's camera innovations have truly paid off in this model." CNET also noted how the phone's **AI enhancements** helped improve both **camera quality** and **battery management**, contributing to a more seamless user experience.

CNET's reviewers also lauded the **S25 Ultra's design**, calling it "sleek, modern, and functional." The **titanium**

frame and **Gorilla Armor 2 glass** were highlighted as features that give the device a premium feel, while the **IP68 rating** ensures that it can withstand the elements. "It's a phone built for the future," the review stated.

8.3 User Testimonials

The feedback from users of the **Samsung Galaxy S25 Ultra** has been overwhelmingly positive, with many praising its **performance, camera system, battery life**, and **overall user experience**. In this section, we'll examine user testimonials to get a sense of how the **S25 Ultra** is performing in the hands of everyday users.

User Feedback on Performance

"I've been using Samsung smartphones for years, but the **S25 Ultra** blows everything else out of the water. The speed and responsiveness are incredible, even when I'm running multiple apps or playing heavy games. The **Snapdragon 8 Elite processor** really delivers, and the **12GB of RAM** makes multitasking feel effortless. I've never had a smoother experience on a smartphone."

– **Tom R.**, Professional Gamer and Content Creator

Many users echo Tom's sentiments, praising the **S25 Ultra's** ability to handle even the most demanding tasks. The **AI-**

powered performance optimizations have been especially appreciated, with users noting that the device stays fast and responsive over time, even after extended use.

Camera System Praise

"I'm a photography enthusiast, and the **S25 Ultra's** camera is hands down the best I've ever used on a smartphone. The **200MP camera** captures so much detail, and the colors are incredibly vibrant. Even in low light, I'm impressed by how much detail is retained. Plus, the **5x optical zoom** means I can get up close to my subject without losing any quality."

– **Sarah L.**, Professional Photographer

The **S25 Ultra's** camera has been met with universal acclaim from users who value high-quality photos and videos. Many professional photographers and content creators have found that the **200MP wide-angle lens**, combined with **AI enhancements** and **night mode**, provides them with an invaluable tool for capturing stunning images in a wide variety of conditions.

Battery Life and Charging

"I'm always on the go, and the **S25 Ultra**'s battery life is a game-changer for me. I don't have to worry about constantly charging my phone, even when I'm traveling or at work all day. The **45W fast charging** is a lifesaver, too. I can get a quick boost when I need it without waiting around."

– **David M.**, Business Executive

Users consistently praise the **5000mAh battery** and **45W wired charging** as standout features of the **S25 Ultra**. Many users report that they can easily make it through a full day of use without needing to recharge, and the fast-charging capabilities are highly valued for quick top-ups during busy days.

Overall User Experience

"The **S25 Ultra** is by far the best smartphone I've ever owned. It's fast, reliable, and has an amazing camera system. The **AI features** make my experience even better, especially when it comes to managing battery life and taking pictures. It's a bit expensive, but the value you get with all the features is well worth it."

– **Jessica H.**, Tech Enthusiast

Jessica's review represents the general consensus among users who appreciate the **S25 Ultra**'s **premium build quality**, **performance**, and **AI-driven features**. While some users have noted that the device's price is on the higher end, most agree that the **features** and **performance** make it a worthwhile investment.

The **Samsung Galaxy S25 Ultra** has received **numerous awards** and accolades from both the tech industry and users worldwide. Industry awards, such as **Best Smartphone of 2025** and **Best Camera Technology**, reflect the **exceptional** design, **cutting-edge camera capabilities**, and **powerful performance** of the device. Critical acclaim from leading tech websites such as **TechRadar**, **The Verge**, and **CNET** reinforces the phone's status as one of the best smartphones available today. User testimonials also highlight the **S25 Ultra's fast performance**, **amazing camera system**, and **long-lasting battery life**, making it a favorite among tech enthusiasts, professionals, and everyday users alike. The **S25 Ultra** has firmly established itself as a leader in the smartphone market, and these awards and recognitions serve as a testament to Samsung's commitment to delivering excellence in mobile technology.

CHAPTER 9

Current Challenges and Market Position

The **Samsung Galaxy S25 Ultra** has undoubtedly set a high benchmark for smartphones with its advanced technology, impressive performance, and outstanding camera system. However, like any product in the tech industry, the **S25 Ultra** faces its own set of challenges in the competitive and rapidly evolving smartphone market. From **production and supply chain issues** to fierce **competition**, and the constantly changing **consumer perception**, this chapter will explore the current challenges the **S25 Ultra** faces and how Samsung's position in the market has evolved in response.

9.1 Production and Supply Chain Issues

Despite its immense popularity and technical success, the **Samsung Galaxy S25 Ultra** has not been immune to the **global supply chain disruptions** that have impacted the tech industry in recent years. The **S25 Ultra's** production and availability have been affected by factors ranging from **component shortages** to **logistical hurdles**, which have created challenges in meeting the high demand for the device. While Samsung has made efforts to overcome these obstacles, these issues have influenced the **availability** and **pricing** of the device in certain regions.

Component Shortages

One of the primary reasons behind the **production delays** of the **Galaxy S25 Ultra** is the ongoing global **component shortage** that has plagued the smartphone industry. Critical components, such as **semiconductors**, **displays**, and **camera sensors**, are in high demand, and the **supply chain** has struggled to keep up with the increased demand. This issue was exacerbated by the COVID-19 pandemic, which led to factory shutdowns and production delays.

The **S25 Ultra**, with its advanced **200MP camera**, **Snapdragon 8 Elite processor**, and **high-resolution AMOLED display**, requires a substantial amount of cutting-edge components. As such, sourcing and manufacturing these components has proven difficult, which has led to delayed shipments in certain markets. These delays have been particularly evident in markets such as **Europe** and **North America**, where demand for high-end smartphones like the **S25 Ultra** is at its peak.

Logistical Challenges

In addition to **component shortages, logistical challenges** have also impacted the availability of the **Galaxy S25 Ultra**. The ongoing **global shipping disruptions**, coupled with the high demand for the device, have made it difficult to deliver phones to retailers and consumers on time. Shipping delays, port congestion, and rising costs for **freight services** have affected the overall distribution strategy, which has resulted in limited stock availability in certain regions.

Samsung has acknowledged these issues and has worked closely with its suppliers and logistics partners to find solutions. The company has also focused on **local production** in key markets to mitigate the impact of global shipping disruptions. However, despite these efforts, the **S25 Ultra's** availability remains inconsistent in some regions, especially in markets where demand is particularly high.

Impact on Pricing

The **supply chain issues** have also contributed to **price fluctuations** for the **Galaxy S25 Ultra**. Due to the **higher production costs** associated with sourcing components and the disruptions in manufacturing, the price of the **S25 Ultra** has seen a **slight increase** compared to previous models in some regions. While Samsung has worked to minimize the impact on consumers, the rising cost of materials and logistics has inevitably affected the retail price of the device.

Additionally, the **high demand** for the **S25 Ultra** in key markets has created a sense of scarcity, which has led some retailers to increase the price of the phone in the secondary market. This situation has raised concerns among some consumers who are eager to purchase the device but find it difficult to find it at the standard retail price.

Future Outlook for Production and Supply Chain

Samsung has been proactive in addressing **supply chain disruptions** and has made significant investments to secure the necessary components for the **S25 Ultra** and future devices. As the global supply chain recovers, Samsung is expected to increase its production capacity and streamline logistics to ensure that the **S25 Ultra** remains widely available. In the future, the company may also shift more production to **local markets** to further minimize shipping delays and reduce reliance on global supply chains.

9.2 Competition in the Smartphone Market

The smartphone market is highly competitive, and the **Samsung Galaxy S25 Ultra** is far from being the only high-end flagship on the market. **Apple**, **Google**, and other key players have all released smartphones with similar features, making it essential for Samsung to continually innovate in order to stay ahead of the competition. In this section, we will explore the main competitors of the **S25 Ultra** and how Samsung's device stacks up against them.

Apple iPhone 15 Pro Max

The **Apple iPhone 15 Pro Max** is one of the most direct competitors to the **Samsung Galaxy S25 Ultra**. Apple's flagship smartphone has long been regarded as the industry leader in terms of **performance, camera quality**, and **user experience**. With its own impressive **camera system, A17 Bionic chip**, and **iOS 17** operating system, the **iPhone 15 Pro Max** is a formidable rival to the **S25 Ultra**.

One area where the **iPhone 15 Pro Max** competes directly with the **S25 Ultra** is in the **camera department**. The **iPhone 15 Pro Max** features a **48MP main camera** with advanced **optical zoom capabilities** and improved **low-light performance**. Apple's camera system has long been praised for its **color accuracy** and **natural-looking photos**, making it a preferred choice for many users, especially in the **portrait photography** and **video recording** areas.

Additionally, **Apple's ecosystem** continues to be a strong selling point for many consumers. The seamless integration between the **iPhone 15 Pro Max** and other Apple products, such as **MacBooks**, **Apple Watches**, and **iPads**, makes it a compelling option for users who are already invested in the Apple ecosystem.

Google Pixel 9 Pro

The **Google Pixel 9 Pro** is another competitor in the high-end smartphone market. Known for its **exceptional camera performance**, the **Pixel 9 Pro** is often considered one of the best devices for mobile photography, thanks to its advanced **AI-driven software** and **computational photography** features. Google's focus on **AI** and **machine learning** allows the **Pixel 9 Pro** to deliver stunning images with great detail, particularly in low-light conditions.

While the **Pixel 9 Pro** may not match the **S25 Ultra** in terms of raw hardware specifications, such as the **200MP camera** or **Snapdragon 8 Elite** processor, its **AI-driven features**, **clean Android experience**, and superior **photography capabilities** make it a strong competitor in the premium smartphone market.

Moreover, **Google's integration of Android** allows for a **pure Android experience** without the bloatware and customizations found in other manufacturers' devices. This simplicity and focus on software optimization have made the

Pixel series a popular choice for Android purists and those who prioritize software over hardware.

Xiaomi Mi 14 Ultra

Xiaomi, a Chinese smartphone manufacturer, has become a significant player in the premium smartphone market. The **Xiaomi Mi 14 Ultra** competes with the **Samsung Galaxy S25 Ultra** by offering similar features at a more competitive price point. The **Mi 14 Ultra** boasts a **200MP camera**, **Snapdragon 8 Gen 3 processor**, and a **120Hz AMOLED display**, making it a direct competitor to Samsung's **S25 Ultra** in terms of hardware specifications.

While Xiaomi offers impressive **hardware** at a more affordable price, it has yet to match Samsung's reputation for **software** and **brand recognition** in many regions. Samsung's well-established **One UI** software, **global customer support**, and integration with other Samsung devices give it an edge over Xiaomi in terms of user experience and reliability.

Oppo Find X6 Pro

Oppo, another Chinese brand, has risen in prominence due to its high-end smartphones that often offer similar specifications to Samsung and Apple devices but at a more competitive price. The **Oppo Find X6 Pro** is a premium device that rivals the **S25 Ultra** with its **50MP main camera**, **100W fast charging**, and **6.7-inch AMOLED display**.

While **Oppo** has made significant strides in the premium market, its global reach and brand recognition still lag behind Samsung's. However, its competitive pricing and innovative features make it a strong contender in regions where Samsung is not as dominant, particularly in **Asia** and parts of **Europe**.

9.3 Consumer Perception and Feedback

Consumer feedback is a crucial factor in determining the long-term success of any device. While the **Samsung Galaxy S25 Ultra** has been met with overall praise, there are areas where users have voiced concerns or offered constructive criticism. In this section, we will explore the general consumer perception of the **S25 Ultra**, focusing on both the positive feedback and the criticisms.

Positive Consumer Feedback

The **Samsung Galaxy S25 Ultra** has received a great deal of positive feedback from consumers who have praised its **camera performance**, **overall design**, and **exceptional**

display. Many users have expressed satisfaction with the **200MP camera**, highlighting its ability to capture incredibly detailed images even in challenging lighting conditions. The **5x optical zoom** and **AI enhancements** have also been praised for delivering sharp, vibrant images.

Consumers have also commended the **performance** of the device, with many noting the **Snapdragon 8 Elite processor**'s ability to handle demanding apps and games with ease. The **smooth performance** and **responsive touch screen** have been key selling points for many users, particularly those who rely on their phones for multitasking and productivity.

Another feature that has garnered positive attention is the **display**. Users consistently highlight the **6.9-inch Dynamic LTPO AMOLED 2X display** as one of the best in the smartphone industry, thanks to its stunning colors, high resolution, and smooth refresh rate. Many have also praised the **battery life** and **fast charging capabilities**, with users reporting that they can easily get through a full day on a single charge, even with heavy use.

Criticism and Areas of Improvement

Despite the overwhelming positive response, some users have raised concerns or pointed out areas where the **S25**

Ultra could improve. One of the most common criticisms is the **price**. While the device is undoubtedly packed with **cutting-edge technology**, some users feel that the **S25 Ultra**'s high price point makes it less accessible compared to competitors like **Xiaomi** and **Oppo**, which offer similar features at a more affordable price.

Another issue that has been brought up by users is the **lack of expandable storage**. While the **S25 Ultra** offers generous internal storage options, some users prefer the flexibility of a **microSD card slot** to further expand storage. The absence of this feature has been a point of contention for those who use their phones for media-heavy tasks like photography and video recording.

Additionally, while the **S25 Ultra**'s **AI features** are generally appreciated, some users feel that **Bixby**, Samsung's virtual assistant, still lags behind competitors like **Google Assistant** and **Apple's Siri**. Although **Bixby** has improved over time, some users find it less intuitive and responsive compared to its rivals.

Brand Loyalty and Reputation

Despite some criticisms, the **S25 Ultra** has benefited from strong **brand loyalty** and **positive perception** of Samsung's reputation for quality and innovation. Many Samsung users have remained loyal to the brand because of its **reliable customer service**, **premium build quality**, and the seamless integration between Samsung devices. Consumers who are already embedded within the **Samsung ecosystem**—including wearables, tablets, and smart home devices—often choose the **S25 Ultra** because of the added value of integration and cross-device functionality.

The **Samsung Galaxy S25 Ultra** is a testament to Samsung's commitment to innovation and quality in the smartphone market. Despite facing challenges such as **supply chain issues** and fierce competition from brands like **Apple**, **Google**, and **Xiaomi**, the **S25 Ultra** has been recognized for its **outstanding camera system, powerful performance**, and **stunning display**. While the price remains a point of contention for some, the overall consumer feedback has been overwhelmingly positive, with many praising the device for its **cutting-edge technology** and **premium design**.

As the **smartphone market** continues to evolve, the **S25

CHAPTER 10

The Future of the Galaxy S Series

The **Samsung Galaxy S series** has been one of the most successful and influential product lines in the smartphone industry. From its early beginnings to the **Samsung Galaxy S25 Ultra**, the Galaxy S series has constantly pushed the boundaries of what smartphones can do, offering cutting-edge technology, stunning displays, powerful processors, and impressive cameras. As we look to the future, it's clear that Samsung will continue to innovate, but the direction of its flagship series will evolve in response to changing consumer needs, new technologies, and an increasingly competitive smartphone market. This chapter explores the **anticipated developments** for the **Galaxy S series**, examines **Samsung's strategic direction**, and provides some **closing thoughts** on the future of this iconic product line.

10.1 Anticipated Developments

The **Samsung Galaxy S series** has been at the forefront of smartphone technology, and the **Galaxy S25 Ultra** serves as the pinnacle of the series. However, the future of this flagship line promises to bring even more groundbreaking innovations. In this section, we will explore several **anticipated developments** that are likely to shape the future of the Galaxy S series, including advancements in **camera technology, AI integration, foldable devices, 5G and beyond,** and **sustainability** efforts.

Camera Technology and Computational Photography

One of the most exciting areas of **advancement** in future Galaxy S models is the continued **evolution of camera technology.** The **200MP camera** on the **Galaxy S25 Ultra** is already a game-changer, but it is likely that future Galaxy S devices will take this technology even further. We can expect even **higher resolution sensors,** possibly reaching **400MP** or more, as well as **improved zoom capabilities.** Advances in **optical zoom** and **periscope lenses** will continue to enhance the zooming capabilities of Samsung's flagship devices.

Furthermore, **computational photography** will become even more advanced. Future **Galaxy S** models will likely integrate **AI-driven algorithms** for better low-light performance, more accurate color reproduction, and the ability to automatically adjust settings based on the scene being captured. This could lead to **seamless video-to-photo transitions,** improved **depth mapping,** and enhanced

portrait modes that rival the best DSLR cameras in terms of background blur and subject focus.

The integration of **AI** with the **camera system** will enable further innovations in **real-time processing**, such as **enhanced AR features** that improve how virtual elements interact with real-world environments. Expect Samsung to integrate even more **AR-driven photography** options in future Galaxy S models, allowing users to interact with their photos and videos in ways that haven't been possible before.

AI Integration and Personalization

As **AI technology** continues to evolve, the **Galaxy S series** will become even smarter and more personalized. Samsung has already made significant strides in **AI integration** with **Bixby, AI-powered camera systems**, and **performance optimizations**. The future of the Galaxy S series will likely see deeper integration of **machine learning** and **predictive AI** that will enhance the overall user experience.

Future Galaxy S devices could use AI to **anticipate user behavior** and offer personalized recommendations. For instance, the phone might learn a user's routine and proactively suggest actions, such as automatically silencing notifications during work hours or switching to a **dark mode** when it detects low light in the environment. Additionally,

Samsung could further enhance **AI voice assistants**, making Bixby even more intuitive and capable of understanding natural language and context.

In the realm of **productivity**, Samsung could continue to refine AI-driven task automation, enabling devices to **streamline workflows** by learning what tasks are most commonly performed and offering efficient shortcuts and suggestions. This AI could extend to integrating Galaxy S devices into the **smart home ecosystem**, offering users better control over their environment, from lighting to security.

5G and Beyond: 6G and Future Connectivity

The **Samsung Galaxy S series** is at the forefront of **5G connectivity**, and future iterations of the Galaxy S devices will continue to support faster and more reliable networks. The **S25 Ultra** already takes advantage of **5G speeds**, allowing for faster download speeds, smoother streaming, and improved connectivity for gaming and video calls.

However, **Samsung's vision for the future** goes beyond **5G**. The company is already exploring the **potential of 6G** networks, which are expected to deliver even faster speeds, ultra-low latency, and more reliable connectivity. As **6G technology** matures, future Galaxy S models could offer

unmatched connectivity, supporting **virtual reality (VR)** and **augmented reality (AR)** applications, as well as **massive IoT (Internet of Things) connectivity**.

With **6G**, the Galaxy S series may integrate **advanced cloud computing** capabilities, allowing for **seamless integration with other devices** and **smart environments**. This will transform how users interact with their smartphones, allowing them to stream more data-intensive content, work in virtual spaces, and access cloud-based applications without the need for powerful local hardware.

Foldable Devices and Form Factor Innovation

Another anticipated development for the **Galaxy S series** is the continued evolution of **foldable smartphones**. Samsung has already pioneered the foldable market with devices like the **Galaxy Z Fold** and **Galaxy Z Flip**, but the future of foldable technology within the Galaxy S series is likely to see even more **refined designs** and **innovative features**.

The next generation of foldable Galaxy S devices could have a more **seamless form factor** and **improved durability**, with stronger foldable displays and thinner profiles. Samsung could also incorporate **multi-tasking enhancements**, making it easier for users to utilize the foldable form to run multiple apps simultaneously or engage in productivity tasks with ease.

Additionally, we may see **hybrid devices** that combine the benefits of **foldable screens** with **traditional smartphone designs**. This could include devices that offer the flexibility of a larger screen when unfolded but still maintain the compact size and portability of a traditional smartphone when folded.

Sustainability and Eco-friendly Technology

As consumers become more environmentally conscious, the **Galaxy S series** is expected to embrace more **sustainable practices** in its development. Samsung has already started to integrate **eco-friendly materials** into its smartphones, such as **recycled plastic** and **environmentally friendly packaging**. Future Galaxy S devices will likely continue this trend with even more sustainable components, **solar charging capabilities**, and longer-lasting battery technologies.

Samsung's commitment to **green technology** will likely extend beyond the device itself, with the company incorporating **energy-efficient manufacturing processes** and striving to reduce its carbon footprint throughout the product lifecycle. We can also expect more **recyclable** components, allowing consumers to more easily recycle their devices when they are ready to upgrade to a newer model.

10.2 Samsung's Strategic Direction

Looking forward, Samsung is focused on expanding its **global dominance** in the smartphone market while also ensuring that its **Galaxy S series** remains at the cutting edge of innovation. As a company, Samsung is pursuing a multifaceted strategic direction to maintain its competitive edge, focusing on **new technologies**, **strategic partnerships**, and **diversification** to build a more sustainable and forward-looking business.

Expanding the Ecosystem

One of the key strategies for Samsung moving forward is to expand and strengthen its **ecosystem of devices**. Samsung has already established a strong presence in areas such as **smartphones, smartwatches, tablets, laptops**, and **smart home devices**. The company's **SmartThings platform** is a central hub for smart home integration, and Samsung is working to ensure that all of its products, including the **Galaxy S series**, work seamlessly together.

By creating a more cohesive ecosystem, Samsung aims to provide customers with a unified experience across its range of products. The goal is to make it easier for users to transition between devices, whether it's using a Galaxy S smartphone to control their **smart home devices**, stream media from a **Samsung TV**, or track fitness metrics on a **Samsung Galaxy Watch**.

Samsung's commitment to building this **interconnected ecosystem** also extends to its **partnerships with third-party companies**. Collaborations with **Google, Microsoft,** and **Amazon** have allowed Samsung to integrate their services, such as **Google Assistant, Office 365**, and **Amazon Alexa**, directly into Samsung devices. These partnerships will likely continue, enabling Samsung to further extend its ecosystem and add value to the user experience.

Strengthening Brand Loyalty

Samsung's strategy also focuses on **strengthening brand loyalty** through the development of **exclusive features** and services for Galaxy S users. The **Samsung Galaxy App Store, Samsung Health**, and **Samsung Pay** are all part of this strategy, providing users with a variety of services that can only be fully experienced on a Samsung device. By offering unique services and tools, Samsung hopes to build deeper relationships with customers and make its devices indispensable to their daily lives.

Additionally, Samsung's **Galaxy Upgrade Program**, which allows customers to upgrade to the latest model every year, is an effort to encourage loyalty among users and keep them engaged with the brand over time. This program, along with **trade-in incentives** and **financing options**, helps lower the barrier to entry for consumers looking to upgrade to the latest Galaxy S device.

Emphasis on Artificial Intelligence and 5G

As mentioned earlier, **AI** and **5G connectivity** are central to Samsung's strategy for the future of the **Galaxy S series**. Samsung has already integrated **AI-powered features** into its devices, from the **camera system** to **battery management**, and it will continue to expand on this in the years to come. **AI-based enhancements** are expected to become a defining feature of future Galaxy devices, improving **user experience**, **personalization**, and **automation**.

In addition, Samsung is committed to being at the forefront of **5G** technology. As 5G networks expand globally, Samsung aims to leverage the faster speeds and lower latency of **5G** to offer users enhanced experiences in **gaming**, **video streaming**, **virtual reality**, and **augmented reality**. **6G technology** is already on Samsung's radar, and the company is investing in **next-generation connectivity** to ensure that its devices remain future-proof.

10.3 Closing Thoughts

The **Samsung Galaxy S series** has evolved significantly over the years, becoming one of the most influential and technologically advanced product lines in the smartphone industry. From the **S series' early days** to the current **S25 Ultra**, Samsung has continuously pushed the envelope in terms of **hardware**, **software**, and **user experience**. Looking to the future, it is clear that Samsung will continue to innovate, driven by advances in **AI**, **camera technology**, **5G**, and **sustainability**.

While the **S25 Ultra** represents the pinnacle of Samsung's smartphone development, the company's future devices will likely build upon its success by integrating even more **cutting-edge features** and creating a more **connected ecosystem** of products. Samsung's strategic direction focuses on **expanding its ecosystem**, **enhancing brand loyalty**, and **leading the way in AI and 5G**, ensuring that the Galaxy S series will remain competitive in an ever-evolving market.

As technology continues to advance, Samsung's commitment to innovation will be essential in maintaining its position as a global leader in the smartphone industry. Whether through the next iteration of the **Galaxy S** series or new product categories altogether, Samsung's vision for the future is one of continued excellence, adaptability, and consumer satisfaction. The future of the **Galaxy S series** is bright, and we can expect even more groundbreaking innovations in the years to come.

CONCLUSION

The Samsung Galaxy S25 Ultra – A Benchmark in Smartphone Innovation

The **Samsung Galaxy S25 Ultra** stands as a defining moment in the evolution of smartphones, cementing its place as one of the most innovative and powerful devices in the mobile tech industry. From its **cutting-edge camera system** to its **lightning-fast performance**, the **S25 Ultra** offers an exceptional experience for both casual users and power users alike. Throughout this book, we've explored every aspect of the **Galaxy S25 Ultra**, from its **design and build quality** to its **software**, **performance**, and **camera capabilities**. We've also examined the challenges Samsung faces, its market position, and the future of the Galaxy S series. Now, in this concluding chapter, we will reflect on the key takeaways, highlight the key aspects that make the **S25 Ultra** a standout device, and provide final thoughts on its place in the larger context of the smartphone industry.

A Technological Marvel

At its core, the **Samsung Galaxy S25 Ultra** represents the culmination of years of innovation, research, and development by Samsung. The **S25 Ultra** is a device that goes beyond the ordinary smartphone. It's a **powerful tool** that seamlessly blends **premium design** with **cutting-edge technology**. Samsung's commitment to delivering high-quality products is evident in every aspect of the **S25 Ultra**.

The **S25 Ultra**'s **hardware** is a testament to Samsung's engineering excellence. The **titanium frame**, **Gorilla Armor 2 glass**, and **IP68 water resistance** ensure that the device is both durable and premium in feel. The **6.9-inch Dynamic LTPO AMOLED 2X display** delivers an unmatched visual experience, with **vibrant colors, crystal-clear resolution**, and **120Hz refresh rates** for fluid scrolling and gaming. The addition of **AI-powered performance optimizations** ensures that the device not only looks great but also performs flawlessly, making it one of the fastest and most responsive smartphones available today.

Samsung's commitment to **advanced camera technology** is fully realized in the **S25 Ultra**, where the **200MP primary camera** sets a new standard for mobile photography. The device's ability to capture detailed, vibrant images across various lighting conditions is unparalleled, making it the go-to choice for photography enthusiasts. **AI-powered enhancements**, such as **scene optimization**, **night mode**, and **Super Steady video**, ensure that users can capture breathtaking moments, whether they are in bright daylight or in challenging low-light conditions.

On the software front, the **Galaxy S25 Ultra** runs on **Android 15** and **One UI 7**, providing a user-friendly interface with a focus on simplicity, customization, and seamless integration with the Samsung ecosystem. The integration of **AI features** further enhances the user experience, from improving battery life to offering smarter ways to manage apps and tasks. Samsung's ecosystem, which includes smartwatches, tablets, and home devices, allows for an interconnected experience that few other manufacturers can match.

Challenges Faced by the Galaxy S25 Ultra

While the **S25 Ultra** excels in many areas, it is not without its challenges. As we've seen in previous chapters, **production and supply chain issues** have hindered the device's availability in certain markets. The ongoing global **component shortages** and **shipping disruptions** have caused delays in the manufacturing and distribution of the device, leading to **limited stock availability** in high-demand regions. While Samsung has made efforts to address these challenges, the **global semiconductor shortage** remains a significant issue that continues to affect the entire tech industry, including Samsung's ability to produce flagship smartphones like the **S25 Ultra** in large quantities.

The **price point** of the **S25 Ultra** has also been a point of contention for some consumers. While the device's premium features and capabilities justify the cost for many, the **high price tag** may make the **S25 Ultra** less accessible to some buyers, especially in price-sensitive markets. With fierce competition from brands like **Apple**, **Google**, and **Xiaomi**, who offer similar features at lower prices, Samsung may face challenges in convincing potential buyers to invest in the **S25 Ultra**. The **absence of expandable storage** also remains a drawback for users who prefer the flexibility to increase storage via a microSD card, as many other devices still offer this feature.

Furthermore, while **Bixby**, Samsung's virtual assistant, has made significant improvements over the years, it still lags behind its competitors, such as **Google Assistant** and **Siri**, in terms of user experience and functionality. This is something Samsung will likely need to address in future updates, especially as AI continues to play a central role in smartphone innovation.

The Competitive Landscape

The **Samsung Galaxy S25 Ultra** faces stiff competition from other flagship smartphones in the market. Apple's **iPhone 15 Pro Max** remains a powerful competitor, offering similar performance, exceptional camera capabilities, and a seamless user experience within the Apple ecosystem. While Samsung and Apple continue to battle for dominance in the high-end smartphone market, other players like **Google** and **Xiaomi** are also making significant strides with their flagship devices.

Google's Pixel 9 Pro continues to impress with its AI-powered features and computational photography, making it a strong contender for photography enthusiasts. Similarly, **Xiaomi**'s **Mi 14 Ultra** and **Oppo's Find X6 Pro** offer **cutting-edge features** at more affordable price points, presenting a real challenge to Samsung's high-end offerings.

Despite this, the **Galaxy S25 Ultra** has its own set of unique selling points, including the **200MP camera**, **superior display technology**, and **integration with Samsung's broader ecosystem**. Samsung's ability to offer a premium experience that seamlessly integrates with other Samsung devices, such as **smartwatches, tablets**, and **smart home**

products, gives it an edge over competitors, particularly for users who already own Samsung products.

Consumer Perception and Market Position

Consumer perception of the **Samsung Galaxy S25 Ultra** has generally been overwhelmingly positive, particularly among users who prioritize **camera quality**, **performance**, and **display excellence**. The **S25 Ultra** is seen as a **flagship device** that pushes the boundaries of smartphone technology, offering a premium experience in every aspect. However, there are areas where consumers have expressed concerns, such as the **price**, **lack of expandable storage**, and **the performance of Bixby** as a virtual assistant.

Despite these challenges, Samsung has maintained a strong position in the premium smartphone market, and the **S25 Ultra** has reinforced its reputation as a **premium flagship device**. Samsung has successfully carved out a niche for itself as the leader in **mobile display technology**, **camera innovation**, and **AI integration**. While the **S25 Ultra** may face competition from other top-tier devices, Samsung's ability to consistently innovate ensures that it will continue to be a leader in the market for years to come.

Looking ahead, Samsung's continued focus on **AI-driven enhancements**, **5G** capabilities, and **sustainability** will likely keep the Galaxy S series at the forefront of the smartphone industry. With its **cutting-edge camera system, superb display,** and **powerful performance,** the **S25 Ultra** will continue to be a top contender in the premium smartphone space, and the future iterations of the Galaxy S series will only build on this foundation.

Samsung's Strategic Direction

Samsung's **strategic direction** in the smartphone market revolves around creating a **seamless ecosystem** that connects its devices, from smartphones to smartwatches, TVs, and home appliances. The **S25 Ultra** represents a key component of this ecosystem, providing users with a unified experience that is not limited to just a smartphone. By focusing on **AI integration, connectivity,** and **smart home functionality,** Samsung is positioning itself as a leader in the broader **technology ecosystem.**

In addition, Samsung is focusing on **sustainability** with the introduction of eco-friendly materials, energy-efficient manufacturing processes, and the promotion of **recycling programs** for old devices. This focus on sustainability is increasingly important as consumers become more environmentally conscious and demand **greener alternatives** from tech companies.

The Future of the Galaxy S Series

As we look to the future, the **Galaxy S series** is likely to continue evolving in exciting ways. The **S25 Ultra** has set a high bar for what a flagship smartphone should offer, and future devices in the series will undoubtedly raise the stakes even higher. With advancements in **camera technology**, **AI**, and **connectivity**, Samsung's future flagship models will likely redefine what is possible in mobile technology.

Moreover, Samsung's exploration of **foldable devices** and **hybrid form factors** indicates that the company will continue to experiment with new designs and technologies. We can expect future Galaxy S models to incorporate **foldable screens**, **enhanced AI capabilities**, and **next-gen 5G** support, ensuring that the Galaxy S series remains a **pioneering force** in the mobile tech industry.

Final Thoughts

The **Samsung Galaxy S25 Ultra** is a landmark device in the smartphone industry, representing the pinnacle of what modern smartphones can achieve in terms of **performance**, **camera quality**, **design**, and **innovation**. It is a **premium flagship** that delivers on its promises, offering users an exceptional experience in every regard. While there are challenges that Samsung must continue to navigate—such as production issues, pricing concerns, and competition from other brands—the **S25 Ultra** has undoubtedly set the stage for future smartphones and reaffirmed Samsung's position as a leader in the mobile tech industry.

Looking ahead, the **Galaxy S series** will undoubtedly continue to evolve, embracing new technologies and innovations that will shape the future of mobile technology. Samsung's focus on **AI**, **5G**, **sustainability**, and **ecosystem integration** ensures that its devices will remain relevant and competitive in the years to come. For now, the **S25 Ultra** stands as a testament to Samsung's commitment to delivering cutting-edge, world-class smartphones that push the boundaries of what is possible.

As the smartphone market continues to evolve, the **Samsung Galaxy S series** will undoubtedly continue to lead the charge, offering users a glimpse into the future of mobile technology with each new release. The **S25 Ultra** is not just a smartphone—it is a glimpse of what the future holds.

www.ingramcontent.com/pod-product-compliance
Lightning Source LLC
LaVergne TN
LVHW051659050326
832903LV00032B/3909